Mr. Funny Pants

Mr. Funny Pants

Michael Showalter

GRAND CENTRAL
PUBLISHING

NEW YORK   BOSTON

Grand Central Publishing
Hachette Book Group
237 Park Avenue
New York, NY 10017

www.HachetteBookGroup.com

Printed in the United States of America

First Edition: February 2011
10 9 8 7 6 5 4 3 2 1

Grand Central Publishing is a division of Hachette Book Group, Inc.
The Grand Central Publishing name and logo is a trademark of Hachette Book Group, Inc.

Library of Congress Cataloging-in-Publication Data

Showalter, Michael.
    Mr. funny pants / Michael Showalter. — 1st ed.
      p. cm.
    ISBN 978-0-446-54210-4
    1. Showalter, Michael, 1970–   2. American wit and humor.   3. Comedians—United States—Biography.   I. Title.
      PN2287.S374A3 2011
      792.7'6028092—dc22
      [B]   2010019302

"Hey! Mr. Tambourine Man, play a song for me"
 —Bob Dylan

"Don't shoot 'til you see the whites of their eyes!"
 —General Prescott

"It ain't the size of the boat that counts. It's the motion of the ocean."
 —my old high school friend Richard

For Amelia, my lovely wife of forty years. Tobias and Evelyn, my beautiful children. Scooter, my chocolate Labrador, and all seventeen of our chickens at our farm that we have. This book is for you.

About the Author

- Hometown: Princeton, New Jersey (for more, see "About New Jersey," p. xiv)
- Currently Resides: Brooklyn, New York (for more, see "About Brooklyn," p. xvi)
- Age: In years, 40; emotional maturity, 17; physical maturity, 92; spiritual maturity, "Monk-like"
- Marital Status: Hitched
- Occupation: Comedian (oy)
- Favorite Color: Magenta—it's like *magic* + *polenta*
- Favorite Word: Twine—it's like *magic* + *twine* – *magic*
- Least Favorite Word: *Juices* (*Juice* singular I have no problem with)
- Second Least Favorite Word: *Sauce*
- Third Least Favorite Word: *Broth*
- Fourth Least Favorite Word: *Marinate*
- Fifth Least Favorite Word: *Gravy*
- All-Time Least Favorite Couplet of Words: *Sex juices* (see also *Sex gravy* or *Sex broth*)
- Favorite Saying: "I'm plumb tuckered out."
- Favorite Phrase: "Apropos of nothing"
- Favorite Proverb: "The early bird gets the worm."
- First Least Favorite Oft-Heard Saying: "For shits and giggles."
- Second Least Favorite Oft-Heard Saying: "I wake up at the butt-crack of dawn."

- Third Least Favorite Oft-Heard Saying: "That's ridonkulous!"
- Favorite Food: Stuffing
- Least Favorite Food: Lard
- Favorite Type of Pen: Felt-tip
- Least Favorite Type of Pen: Quill (gets ink all over my hands, plus feather breaks easily)
- Favorite Article of Clothing: Sweater
- Least Favorite Article of Clothing: Sweaty sweater
- Favorite Movie: Anything with zombies
- Favorite TV Show: Anything with the words *Project* or *Top* in the title
- Least Favorite TV Show: *Dog Whisperer* (he does NO whispering! WTF!?)
- Biggest Fear: Penis falls off
- Second-Biggest Fear: Gets stuck in Ikea and can't get out
- Greatest Dream: I become a ball of light and float off into orbit.
- Favorite Cities: Paris, Istanbul, and Prague
- Actual Favorite Cities: New York, Boston, and Philly
- Favorite Band: The Velvet Underground
- Actual Favorite Band: The Police
- Biggest Planet: Neptune (not sure if this is true)
- Smallest Planet: Io, Jupiter's largest moon (prob not even a planet)
- Favorite Author: F. Scott Fitzgerald
- Actual Favorite Author: John Grisham
- Truthful Actual Favorite Author: Sports section

Aboot the Author
(For Canadian Edition)

- Favorite Color: Whatever the color of maple syrup is
- Favorite Word: *Aboot* (it's *about* but said differently)
- Least Favorite Word: *About*
- Favorite Prime Minister of Canada: Garry Trudeau
- Favorite Comedy Duo from Canada: Bob and Doug McKenzie
- Second-Favorite Comedy Duo from Canada: N/A
- Third-Favorite Comedy Duo from Canada: N/A
- Most Successful Band from Canada: Nickelback
- Favorite Nickelback Song: N/A
- Favorite Canadian Food: Peameal bacon (back bacon rolled in cornmeal!)
- Second-Favorite Canadian Food: Poutine (French fries covered in cheese curds and gravy!)
- Third-Favorite Canadian Food: Pemmican (According to Wikipedia: prepared from the lean meat of buffalo, elk, or deer. The meat is cut in thin slices and dried over a slow fire until it is hard and brittle. Then it is pounded into very small pieces using stones. The pounded meat is mixed with melted fat. In some cases, dried fruits such as saskatoon berries, cranberries, blueberries, or chokecherries are pounded into powder and then added to the

meat/fat mixture. The resulting mixture is then packed into "green" rawhide pouches for storage.)

Notably Unappetizing Excerpts from the Above Recipe: 1) "until *hard* and *brittle*"; 2) "*pounded* into small pieces"; 3) "melted fat"; 4) "pounded meat"; 5) "saskatoon berries"; 6) "chokecherries"; 7) "rawhide pouches." Or, to put it another way, "most of it."

About Bea Arthur

Beatrice "Bea" Arthur (1922–2009) was a Tony Award–winning and two-time Emmy Award–winning American comedian, actress, and singer. With a career spanning seven decades, Arthur is perhaps best remembered for her trademark role as the title character, Maude Findlay, on the 1970s sitcom *Maude* and for playing Dorothy Zbornak, the divorced substitute teacher on *The Golden Girls*.

About New Jersey

Let's start with the basics:

- Bruce Springsteen is from there and Bon Jovi is too.
- It's got lots of malls and factories in it.
- Typical response to telling someone you're from New Jersey is "Really? What exit?"

Now let's get into the nitty-gritty:

- New Jersey was the eighth state of the Union. This happened all the way back in the 1700s. The 1700s were when George Washington and those guys were doing their thing. For the real history buffs—the first seven states in the Union were (in no particular order):
  - Virginia
  - Wisconsin
  - Peru
  - Dakotas
  - Bears?
  - Virginia again
  - Burlington, Vermont

- The New Jersey State Flower is the hibiscus. (The hibiscus is the first flower I thought of after writing the first part of the sentence "The

New Jersey State Flower is…" Truth be told, I am not 100 percent sure that a hibiscus is even a flower. My spell-check didn't correct the spelling, though, so I know it is, at very least, a real word.)

• The New Jersey State Motto is "You gotta be kiddin' me, bro!" This is said with a thick Jersey accent and is often followed by a flurry of fisticuffs, the sound of cop cars heading to the scene, girlfriends screaming, "No, Danny! We wuz just talkin'! Don't hit him! It ain't worth it!"

• New Jersey is known as the Garden State. This is because gardens are mandatory in New Jersey. If you don't have a garden, you get a $1,500 fine. And if you don't have a garden after already not having a garden, then you will go to jail for a long, long time.

I am from Princeton, New Jersey. Here's a little more about that:
• Princeton is the name of an Ivy League university but also the name of the town that the Ivy League university is in. Princeton is the only Ivy League school named after the town that it is in (with the exception of Yale). Many people don't know about Yale, Connecticut. And there's a reason for that. I lied. It doesn't exist. Princeton's the only one.

• Aaron Burr is buried in Princeton. Aaron Burr was either killed by Alexander Hamilton in a duel or he killed Alexander Hamilton in a duel. I can't remember which one and I promised myself I wouldn't do much research in this section of the book.

• The band Blues Traveler is from Princeton. I was in choir with John Popper and one time he picked me up and dropped me on my head and I had a sore neck after that.

About Brooklyn

- Brooklyn is home to many famous authors, dead and alive. The author of this book considers himself totally equal to, if not way better than, the other famous authors who live here, have lived here, have ever even heard of it. Here is a short list of authors living in Brooklyn who I think that I am equal to or better than:

1. Jonathan Lethem
2. Jonathan Safran Foer
3. Walt Whitman

In particular, I feel like I'm equal to or better than Walt Whitman.

- Brooklyn is well known as the place where the Brooklyn Dodgers started. The Brooklyn Dodgers moved to Los Angeles (like everybody else), sold out, and became the Los Angeles Dodgers. The Brooklyn Dodgers were called the Dodgers because they "dodged" things.

- Brooklyn is considered the "New Manhattan." The "Old Manhattan" ironically isn't Manhattan. The "Old Manhattan" is Tucson, Arizona. (For more facts on "Tucson, Arizona," google "Tucson + Arizona + Facts.")

There are many neighborhoods to Brooklyn. Here is a guide:

Brooklyn Heights: This is where I live. Brooklyn Heights is by far the coolest neighborhood in Brooklyn. Really, really cool people live here. Brooklyn Heights is very quiet and very cool.

Park Slope: Park Slope looks a lot like Brooklyn Heights but tilted, and it's near Prospect Park. That's why it's called Park Slope. It's near a park and it's on a slope. Ironically, there's never anywhere to park your car in Park Slope. For that reason it should really be called "Nowhere to Park Slope."

Fort Greene: Fort Greene is very cool. Lots of really cool black people live in Fort Greene. That's probably a racist thing to say but it's true.

Cobble Hill: Cobble Hill also looks like Brooklyn Heights. The problem with Cobble Hill is that there are too many young parents pushing babies around in prams. They think they're better than everybody just because they are participants in the miracle of life.

Williamsburg: This is where all the hipsters and all the bands are. Williamsburg is in a totally different part of Brooklyn. Williamsburg is pretty run-down. It's got lots of warehouses and loft buildings. It's very industrial. It's kind of like going to Disneyland but instead of cartoon animals it's lots of girls with bangs and bearded young men, all wearing really tight jeans and uncomfortable shoes.

Acknowledgments

I acknowledge that I am writing a book. I also acknowledge that you are, at very least, reading this section of my book. I acknowledge that this sentence you are now reading was ghostwritten by a friend. I acknowledge that by acknowledging that it was ghostwritten it is now no longer ghostwritten because I admitted that it was ghostwritten, which means it's not a secret anymore. I acknowledge that just because it's no longer "ghostwritten" doesn't mean that I wrote it. I did not write it. My friend wrote it. Therefore, the third sentence in this paragraph must be credited to my friend, but because it's ghostwritten, he doesn't want credit. This is the definition of a paradox. I acknowledge that, in fact, this: PARADOX: A *statement that contradicts itself* is the actual definition of *paradox*. I acknowledge that, as a result of having OCD, I am compelled to make this paragraph a little bit longer, even though I can't think of anything else to say. I acknowledge that my editor told me that it didn't *need* to be longer. He even said that no acknowledgments at all would have been fine too. I acknowledge that I told him to shove it up his butt and threatened a lawsuit. He laughed at me and hung up the phone.

Table of Contents

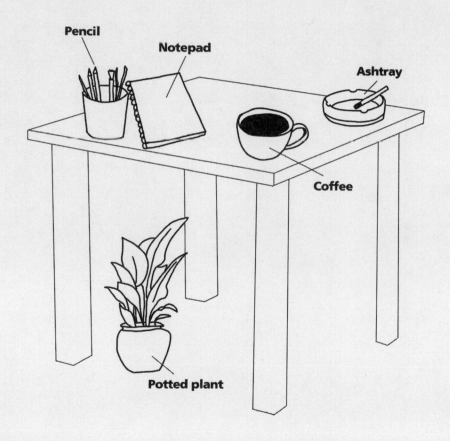

Pencil

Notepad

Ashtray

Coffee

Potted plant

Preface

I know that if I am going to write a book, the first thing I'll need to write is a preface. I don't really understand what purpose this preface will serve, but I know that lots of books start with them, so mine will too.

With that, I opened a new document on my desktop, titled it "Preface," and started writing my book:

PREFACE

When I look back on the experience of writing this book, I am amazed by how different the end product is from what I originally intended. I am so grateful that four years and five continents later I'm still in one piece to write this preface. I couldn't have done it without all of my graduate students, who stayed up late with me so many nights eating bad Chinese takeout on the floor of my new condo in Boston, surrounded by unpacked boxes. My travels through the Middle East were brutal....

At this point, I stopped writing my preface and took a step back. How could I possibly write a preface to a book that wasn't written yet? Who were these "graduate students"? I have no condo in Boston. And why was I saying that I'd traveled through the Middle East? I asked a writer friend of mine (Malcolm Gladwell, if you must know), "What's a preface?" Malcolm said, "Use the preface to explain to your readers how you see your book." Thanks, Malcolm![1]

HOW I SEE THIS BOOK

How do I see this book? Well, let's start with the obvious:

- I see it with my eyes.
- I also "see" it with my hands but if and only if I'm blind and read Braille.
- I take that back. I could also see it with my hands if I knew how to read Braille but wasn't blind.

To Conclude: Reading Braille is one very good way to "see" it with my hands (and by *hands*, I really mean *fingers*).

Another way to "see" the book with my hands would be to have eyes on my hands. If this were true, then I wouldn't need the quotation marks around the word *see* because I'd literally *see* the words with my hands-eyes. Okay, full disclosure: I don't have eyes on my hands.

More than anything, I see this book as a "quilt." It's a patchwork quilt of memories, thoughts, observations, and recollections from my life, imagined or otherwise. To the extent that this last sentence made sense, I thought it was a really well-written line. I especially liked the part where I used the word *patchwork*.

Before committing to the "patchwork quilt" template, I considered many other "blanket templates." For weeks I saw the book as something of a "duvet." This worked for some time, but ultimately I realized that a duvet has certain limitations when used as a framework for writing a full-length book—primary among them the two do not, in any way, relate to each other. (See "book/duvet" comparison that follows.)

---

1. This is a lie—the first of many. I do not know Malcolm Gladwell. (I mean, I know *of* him. I just don't, like, *know* him know him.)

DUVET VS. BOOK COMPARISON	
• Duvet keeps you warm.	• Book doesn't keep you warm. (If you light it on fire, book can keep you warm, but then technically it's not a book anymore; it's kindling.[2])
• Duvet is soft.	• Book is hard . . . until it comes out in paperback. Even when it comes out in paperback, it's still not exactly "soft." It's just less hard than it was before.
• Duvet helps you fall asleep.	• Book also helps you fall asleep. There is, however, one major addendum to this point: Book does not help you fall asleep if book is a "page-turner." Then it actually prevents you from sleeping. The next day you complain to your coworkers that you're "so tired" because you were up all night "engrossed" in a "total" page-turner.

Other blanket templates that I tried were:

- Sleeping bag
- Area rug (not technically a blanket)
- Flannel sheet
- Afghan
- Security blanket
- Snuggie

2. *Kindling* is a collection of easily combustible small sticks or twigs used for starting a fire. Not to be confused with *crackling*, which is the crisp, fatty skin of a roasted pig used for starting a tummy ache, but it's pretty delicious.

None of these quite worked, so I spoke to my editor, Ben, who had two suggestions for me. One suggestion was excellent: "Try patchwork quilt as a template." The other was unbelievably stupid. He said, "Consider the possibility that your book doesn't need to be modeled after a genre of blanket," adding, "There are many other templates for a book besides 'Patchwork quilt.'" I said, "Name one!" He rattled off ten, and, to his credit, none of them were blanket related.

Malcolm's suggestion was only getting me so far, so I decided to take a new approach. Instead of using the preface to tell the reader how I see the book, I decided to tell them how I *don't* see the book. I'm kind of an out-of-the-box thinker. Not to toot my own horn but I am. Apropos of nothing, my own horn is a flugelhorn. The flugelhorn is a distant cousin of the bugle.

HOW DON'T I SEE THIS BOOK?

Again, let's begin with the obvious. *I don't see this book when I am not looking at it.* I repeat: I do not see this book at any moment when I am not looking at it. Furthermore, sometimes I am looking at it, but I'm not really "seeing" it because I'm thinking about something else. Like just the other day, I was looking at the book but thinking about something else. In truth, I was thinking about sex. I don't feel the need to go into gory detail, but it involved blowjobs. You know, inserting your penis into a woman's mouth, at which point your penis becomes engorged with blood or, more colloquially, "hard," as said woman slobbers on it. I mean, I suppose *slobber* isn't the right word. That makes it sound dirty. It wasn't dirty. It was exotic. It was mutual. I chomped her box. We were young, barely in our twenties. And we were in Corsica and we barely knew each other. I mean, we were boyfriend and girlfriend. It wasn't a random thing, but in the bigger scope of "knowing someone" we barely knew each other; let's be honest, we barely knew ourselves. And either way, that's what you do when you're in Corsica. You make love. I mean, sure there's the Napoleon Bonaparte museum and windsurfing. And we did those things, but mostly we stayed in the hotel room because we were shrooming and we were too afraid to go out onto the street, and... anyway. Like I said, I don't want to go into gory detail.

In conclusion, being that I haven't started to write this book yet, I think it's irresponsible of me to write the preface first. So it is with great regret that I ask you to *unread* this chapter. The best way to unread this would be to have your memory erased.

Post-Preface

The post-preface is a brand-new book feature that is getting a lot of "play" these days. All the big authors are doing it: Stephen King, Mike Chabon, Anne Rice. They all do it.

I am hoping that fifty years from now, when all writers employ an "author's post-preface," they will say, "Michael Showalter was a part of that vanguard." Just like when Thomas Edison's name is mentioned, people say, "He invented English muffins. Thomas's English Muffins."

I considered doing a "pre-post-preface" because I'm told that's all the rage with "up-and-comers." This would have come after the preface and before the post-preface, but then I realized that this was still just the preface. Still, I think that the pre-post-preface has potential, so I'm going to stick with it.

At my editor's behest (is *behest* a word?), I also tried to do armnotes instead of footnotes. The idea was to have my footnotes on the left and right margins of the page, just like arms are on the right and left sides of the body. I tried it—even added little "fingernotes" to it. This proved cumbersome and difficult to format.

These were good ideas but as they say, "The best intentions of mice and men." And when I say "they" I don't know who I'm referring to, nor do I know how the quote applies in this situation, but I'm certain it does.[3]

3. Did some research. Now I'm even more confused. It's a quote from a poem by Robert Burns that goes, "The best laid schemes o' mice an' men / Gang aft agley." "*Gang aft agley*"? WTF? It's like he got drunk at the very end of his own poem and started to slur his words or something.

Post-Post-Preface

After much deliberation, I have decided to write a post-post-preface. What's scary about this is that I've written a post-post-preface without also creating its logical corollary, a pre-post-preface. I'm not sure if I did the right thing here, and I'm worried that history will judge me poorly for it. Still, this is a risk that I am willing to take because I believe in the concept of a post-post-preface, and while I fear that I have opened a Pandora's box, I also feel like I'm doing what is right.

> A **Pandora's box** is a box (presumably belonging to someone named Pandora) that, when opened, creates unwarranted complications, due to the fact that her box should never have been opened in the first place. Basically, don't mess with her box. Leave her box alone.

The questions that I am struggling with here are:

- Does this now mean that I need to do a post-post-post-preface?
- Or, even worse, do I need to write a pre-post-post-preface? (And if this is the case, then that means there's a section of my book missing.)

In the interest of being thorough, I will do the pre-post-post-preface next, even though I should have done it before the post-post-preface.

Pre-Post-Post-Preface

I take a medication that helps me with my OCD. It's a generic form of the brand-name prescription drug Zoloft, and I take a very low daily dose of it. That said, sometimes I feel like I should take a higher dose, because if I don't, then I get stuck in a spiral of obsession/compulsion that leads me to do unnecessary and foolish things like writing a "pre-post-post-preface." I still stand by the post-preface, though. The post-preface is revolutionary and will become standard for all books. Still, the bigger issue for me right now is how to wriggle free of the spiral I'm in. In other words, how do I end the pre-post-post-preface? Furthermore, am I now required to return to my post-post-preface and finish that too? I think that the only way to end this is to create a new section altogether.

End of Pre- and Post-Prefaces Preface

Thus concludes the pre- and post-prefaces section of this book. On the following page, you will find page one of the book proper. If you have any questions about the book that weren't adequately addressed in the pre- and post-prefaces, please refer to the "FAQs (Frequently Asked Questions)" on p. 250.

Introduction

My parents got married a year after they met. It would have been very strange had they been married the year *before* they met. My dad taught French at Princeton and then Rutgers and my mom taught English at Rutgers and then Princeton. Strangely enough, my father's first name is English but he teaches French. My mom teaches English but her first name is Elaine, not French. Apropos of nothing, Rutgers, like the word *orange*, does not rhyme with anything.

My sister was born in 1965. Her name is Vinca, as in the French flower *le vinca*.

I was born in 1970. My name is Michael, as in boring first name that every other guy with a penis has. Of course, all guys have a penis, so what I said is redundant. It's just that a penis is sort of that *thing* that makes a guy a *guy*. Right? Like, if he had a vagina he'd be a she. And if he didn't have a penis or a vagina, he'd either be a mannequin or a robot. Then again, I'm sure there's a robot with a working penis out there somewhere. Either way, Michael isn't a very original name—which leads me to believe I was named on a lark.

Here is a short scene of what I imagine it was like when my parents named me.

"What should we call it?" says my dad.

"Uh, I dunno. How about call it...uh...Mike?" says my mom.

"Call it Michael?" asks Dad.

"Mike. Michael. Whichever," says Mom.

"Sure," says Dad.

"Great. Let's go get lunch," says Mom.

"Cool. Sandwiches?" asks Dad.

"Sandwiches. Yes," says Mom.

Cut to thirty-seven years later: One morning, while checking my email, listening to *Vespertine* by Bjork on constant repeat, sipping a mug of coffee, and reading up on the latest news regarding the upcoming presidential election, I received an email from Ben Greenberg, a book editor. He mentioned as a way of breaking the ice that we had some mutual friends, and asked if I had any interest in writing a book.

This raised my hackles.[4] He said he was familiar with my TV and film work and had read some of my writing. In particular, he referenced something I had written about taking ecstasy in my mid-twenties and peeing on myself.

I responded to Ben that I was flattered that he would think of me for such a project. I told him that it was an "intriguing" offer and that I would like a few days to "mull it over." I told him that I was very busy with my "studies" and that after my "mulling it over" period, if I accepted his offer, we'd have to discuss money immediately. I wasn't actually studying anything but it seemed like the right thing to say. I told him that I didn't work cheap and that I expected an unusually high advance for a first-time author, the kind of advance that would make headlines in book industry trade magazines.

Beginning with the sentence "I think there's been a misunderstanding," Ben promptly responded by email to say that no offer had been made yet. He used phrases like "absolutely no guarantees whatsoever," "long shot," and "very unlikely." He explained that I would have to come up with a well-thought-out book proposal that outlined what kind of book I would write and who would read it. I should also attach sample

---

4. A hackle is a long, slender feather on the neck of a male goose. I don't actually have any long feathers on my neck. It's a figure of speech. Moreover, I'm not a goose. I like geese, don't get me wrong. I like them a lot. I'm just not one myself.

pages of writing (see p. 8 for "Book Proposal"). He said that he would then have to take the proposal to his higher-ups and then they would have to sign off on the project before any offer could be made. He also mentioned that I should have low expectations regarding the advance, should an offer even ever come.

Sensing a shift in the power dynamic, fearing that I'd mishandled things, I immediately responded that in the time between my first email and this one, I had had time to mull things over, that I had decided that I really wanted to pursue the project, and that I was desperate for work. I told him not to worry about money at all and that I would pretty much work for free.

He responded that he was "happy" that I was going to pursue the project and that hopefully it would "work out."

I immediately responded that I hoped it would work out too, and then I reiterated that I was more or less desperate for the opportunity and that it really didn't matter what they paid me.

A few hours later he responded that I shouldn't obsess over the money part. He said that if they acquire the book they would definitely pay me but that the more important thing was to just put the proposal together. He encouraged me to just get to work, to please stop emailing him, and worry about the details later. In a postscript he reiterated that I please stop emailing. He almost seemed annoyed.

Ignoring his request, I immediately responded that I wasn't obsessing over the money part and that I would start working on the proposal that very instant and that I was incredibly "jazzed" about the whole venture.

After sending the email, I agonized over my use of the word *jazzed* and wished there was some way that I could take the email back, but I knew it was too late.

I considered sending him another email apologizing for having said the word *jazzed* but I knew that would only remind him that I'd said it in the first place. There was always a chance that he might have forgotten or not noticed.

A few days later, he responded that he was "glad" that I was excited and that he was "looking forward" to seeing what I came up with. He also pointed out that I should take my time and that he'd probably be less available to answer emails for a little while.

I immediately responded that I totally agreed with him about taking my time and that it was "no biggie" at all about not responding sooner to my last email and that I'd be sending him something hopefully by the end of the week.

He didn't respond.

Taking Ecstasy and Peeing on Myself

No drug has a higher "potential to not work" quotient than ecstasy. The first time I did ecstasy nothing happened. After I took it, I waited around for a while for something to happen but I didn't feel any different. The person who gave it to me told me that it would work better if I stood on my head, so I stood on my head in five-minute intervals for about three hours. All I got was a head rush. Eventually, I wanted it to work so badly that I just convinced myself I *was* high. I kept telling my friends, "Oh my God! This is the best feeling ever!" In reality, I think I just felt a little drowsy. The next day my friend's drug dealer told him that he'd accidentally given us melatonin, an herbal sleep remedy. Upon reflection, I realized that I felt drowsy because I WAS drowsy.

The second time I did ecstasy I snorted it. Don't ask. All I remember was that I played tennis that day and was "seeing the ball" very well. Also, I had a stuffy nose for two weeks.

The third time I tried ecstasy, something finally happened. I was with my girlfriend at the time and another couple. We touched stuff and told each other how beautiful we were for four hours.

At the end of the night my girlfriend and I tried to have sex but I couldn't get an erection. I had "numb dick." So we decided that I should masturbate. It became a collaborative effort. I was trying to masturbate and she was rooting me on. After an hour of futility I finally felt like I was going to have an orgasm. "Here it comes," I said. She cheered. I came. It was the biggest orgasm I'd ever had. It was like a gallon of sperm was shooting out of me like a hose. It almost felt like I was peeing.

And I was.

I was peeing.

I was peeing all over myself.

As soon as I realized it I screamed, "Ah! I'm peeing all over myself!" My girlfriend ran into the kitchen and got a roll of paper towels. I clutched my penis and ran, knock-kneed, into the bathroom.

After that third time it was never the same. The last time I did ecstasy was on New Year's Eve 1999. I got really drunk, sat in a folding chair all night long, and watched people dance. It wasn't very fun. I knew that it was an artificial high. (See chart below.)

TYPE OF ARTI-FICIAL HIGH	SHOULD BE USED FOR	IS USED FOR	POSSIBLE SIDE EFFECTS
ALCOHOL *(also: mouthwash, tiramisu, spaghetti with vodka sauce, etc.)*	• Enjoyment of taste • Experiencing light buzz • Pleasant social interaction	• Masking pain • Shirking life's responsibilities • Living in a fantasy world (also: avoiding reality)	• Half-eaten sandwich in bed next day • Piles of unopened mail • Having to apologize a lot about what happened last night • Drunk dialing
MARIJUANA *(also: hash, not corned beef, Turkish)*	• Medicinal pain reliever • Getting more "in touch" with yourself	• Regulating sleep and food intake • Listening to songs that play for longer than twelve minutes • Having great ideas that you forget right after having them	• Smelling like a barn • Getting "pothead" voice and sounding like Keanu Reeves when you talk • Dreadlocks but not a Rastafarian

TYPE OF ARTIFICIAL HIGH	SHOULD BE USED FOR	IS USED FOR	POSSIBLE SIDE EFFECTS
HUFFING GLUE (*also: snuffling glue; flumping glue; ruffling glue*)	• Anything that glue would be used for (woodwork, arts and crafts, etc.)	• Killing brain cells and acting stupid • Preventing yourself from having a future	• Gluing your face together • Having glue all over you • "Glue Face"
COFFEE (*also: Coca-Cola; Thai iced tea; Red Bull*)	• Having "conversations" with people about "art" and "politics" and "prose"	• Getting through life	• Pooping • Getting cranky if you don't have coffee • "Coffee Leg"
GOSSIP MAGAZINES (*also: "watercooler conversations"*)	N/A	• Reveling in other people's misfortune • Looking at nekkid photos of famous people	• Learning things will stop • "Gossip Face" • Not being a better person
PORNOGRAPHY (*smut*)	• Masturbation	• Masturbation	• Blindness
GAMBLING (*engaging in high-risk/high-reward activities*)	• Winning money • Having fun • Feeling good about yourself and your place in the world	• Losing money • Losing watches and valuable possessions • Losing everything that you once held dear	• Getting beaten up by a loan shark or bookie • Living in your car • Living under bridge after you pawn your car

Book Proposal Submitted to Grand Central Publishing on February 7, 2008

What is this book about? This book is all about me. Me, me, me! It's about my life story that I want to tell and hopefully people far and wide will want to read all about it. It is a very well-written and moving story. The writing will be considered by readers to have been very original and fresh but not alienating or subversive.

The story starts when I am young, only a small child (ages 0–5). This portion of the book will be short because I don't remember much of it. In it, I will describe:

1. The Miracle of Childbirth (lots and lots of stuff about placenta, probably too much stuff; we can always edit down but I'd rather have too much placenta stuff than not enough)
2. Nursery School (finger painting and crapping in one's pants)
3. Kindergarden (purposely misspelled)
4. Flinging Spaghetti Around the House
5. That one time when Dad broke my arm because he was angry with me (oh wait, that's Stephen King's *The Shining* not my life)

Though this section, ages 0–5, will be short on substance, I do intend to provide scholarly context. The context part will be *very substantive* and *heavily footnoted*.

- The Vietnam War was still in full swing (it was an "unwinnable" war; napalm; and the "Hanoi Hilton")
- The Beatles had just broken up (Paul's "the walrus")
- The Watergate Scandal was breaking in the news and then Dustin Hoffman played Carl in a movie about it called *All the President's Men*.

After that the story continues on, in meticulous detail, to chronicle my adolescence during the 1980s. This was when Ronald Reagan was president, computers became everywhere, and Communism went away (except in Cuba and Vermont). This part will be anecdotal and nostalgic. It will make you misty eyed, and wistful for an easier time. It will really make you think about when you were that age (ages 9–14) because of all the references that I make that you will get (*Sixteen Candles*, Bananarama, and *M*A*S*H*). That section will be roughly 700 pages long. Some chapters that I'm thinking about for that section are:

- "My First Backpack and What Went in It: Pencils, Notepads, Erasers, Rubik's Cube"
- "Stitches on My Face and Wearing a Papoose in the Doctor's Office to Keep Me from Freaking Out and Knocking Surgical Supplies Over"
- "Peer Pressure and That Time I Smoked Oregano Thinking It Was Pot"

Then, in the book, I go to high school. That part is going to be bittersweet, even sad. It will be sad because a girl I really liked dumped me and I tried to cut myself with a penknife. It will deal with all sorts of great high school stuff like:

- Breaking out with acne ("ZITS ARE THE WORST!")
- Hating your parents ("Ugh, you guys are such *squares*!")

- Puking at parties ("I can't believe I barfed in Steve Brixton's mom's sock drawer!")

You will love this part because I will really remind you of that time and you will identify and by identifying you will like it and by liking it you will like the book and by liking the book you will recommend the book and then it will grow exponentially until everyone knows about it and then it's a best seller on the level of a book by [insert name of bestselling author].

After that, I will write about the 1990s, when I was in college, and what that was like. In the college portion of the book, I will tackle such things as:

- Drinking alcohol ("Wow, I can make myself feel this way every single night!")
- What I majored in (BEER!)
- The Joys of Streaking Across the Quad (see p. 100)
- My semester abroad in Paris (wearing berets and horizontally striped shirts; eating baguettes; rolling my own cigarettes, and watching Clint Eastwood films dubbed in French with English subtitles)

This section will be written in a very, very smart way (maybe even too smart) and you will begin to see larger themes emerge that will make you realize that everything is starting to really mean something, and when you see this you will be very impressed with me and with yourself for being clever enough to figure it out. These themes are going to be:

1. Man vs. Society
2. Man vs. Himself
3. Society vs. Himself
4. Himself vs. Himself
5. Society Man vs. Himself/Himself

After the college portion of the book, which will be long and *extremely dense*, I will transition into a lengthy and too-wordy section that I will call "The Roaring Twenties." This is a reference to the historical era of the 1920s but it's a double entendre because it's also about when I was in my twenties. In this section I will talk at length about how I snorted heroin by accident and went skinny-dipping in Lake Washington. I will also talk about how I construct a joke and I will break it down into graphs and charts. This section can serve not only as an interesting look into the craft of comedy but also as a how-to manual for aspiring comedians. I will then go on to deconstruct my own sense of humor in a long and scholarly essay titled "The Comic Sensibility of Michael Showalter: A Study in Contrasts." After this, I will move into my thirties, and I will talk about being depressed. That section will be long, kind of a drag, and frankly, quite boring. In it, I will discuss:

- My panic attacks ("I'm dying! Oh wait, no I'm not. I'm just kind of nervous.")
- My insomnia due to my Restless Leg Syndrome (although Restless Leg comes in handy at a dance party and on the soccer field, I must admit)
- My days when I couldn't get out of bed ("What's the point? I'll only be disappointed by the day.")
- My chronic self-centeredness (being self-centered doesn't make you a bad person; it just means you're self-centered)
- My fear of intimacy ("I'm a lone wolf.")
- My incapacitating fear of people ("This cocktail party is overwhelming me. Everyone is conversing too much. I need some fresh air...oh God...I'm gonna puke.")
- My low self-esteem ("I'm ugly.")
- My obsessive-compulsive disorder ("Must tie my shoes perfectly! This could take all day!")
- My fear of confined spaces ("This elevator is scary!")
- My sense of impending doom ("The End of Days lurks around the corner; oh nope, it's just another Starbucks.")
- Fear of being alone for the rest of my life (sometimes I feel like I'm alone even when I'm not)

- Fear of being punched in the face (you think it will hurt more than it does; being humiliated or rejected is worse)
- Fear of eating improperly canned meats (because then you'll get botulism; botulism is a type of food poisoning caused by a bacterium that grows on improperly canned meats)
- Fear of having food stuck in my teeth (spinach in particular)
- Fear of having food stuck anywhere on body (leg of lamb hanging off of elbow would be mortifying)
- Fear of farting in bed with lover (Lover says, "Did you just fart?" I say, "No! My neighbor plays the tuba sometimes late at night.")
- Fear of bedbugs ("We're moving the fuck out of here!")
- Fear of government institutions ("Taxation without representation!" "54/40 or fight!" "Tippecanoe and Tyler Too!")
- Fear of institutions that fear government institutions (Tea Bag Party)
- Fear of tripping onstage when receiving an award ("Can you believe Showalter wore an evening gown!")
- Fear of never receiving an award ("And the winner is…someone other than Michael Showalter!")
- Fear of being judged ("Let me live my life the way I wanna live it! You worry about your own damn self!")
- Fear of being judged as harshly as I judge other people ("If you think about me the way that I think about you, then I'm in big trouble.")
- Fear of needles ("Doctor, before you prick my finger, would you mind taking me under?")
- Fear of not being understood ("That's not what I'm saying!")
- Fear of not understanding ("What do you mean?!")
- Fear of getting old (don't want to forget things like my own name or my children's names)
- Fear of not growing up (kind of actually do want to forget things, like I want to forget the time that I snorted heroin by accident and went skinny-dipping in Lake Washington)

- Fear of the unknown ("I won't leave the house because I don't know what's out there! There could be zombies out there waiting to eat me out!")
- Fear of the truth ("I am a ball of light, the truth does not exist.")
- Fear of missing out ("Who was at the party?! Did anyone ask about me?")
- Fear of not getting enough sleep ("I'm really tired all the time. What gives?")
- Fear of sleeping too much ("I *have* to get out of this bed and start the day.")
- Fear of sexual impotency ("Maybe I could just sort of mash it in?")
- Fear of sexual addiction ("I need to go to the ER. I've had an erection since last Tuesday and all of my fingers and toes are falling off!")
- Fear of codependency ("I love you! I hate you! Fuck off! Come here! Leave me alone! Hold me!")
- Fear of making decisions ("I don't care where we eat, honey. Just pick something!")
- Fear of making the wrong decision once a decision's been made ("I don't want sushi. Pick something else.")
- Fear of things changing ("I'm feeling different right now. That scares me.")
- Fear of things staying the same ("I want to feel different. I crave change.")
- Fear of the sun (vampires)
- Fear of the moon (werewolves)
- Fear of zombies (zombies)

Here I might answer the question "What is a 'zombie'?" Well, the word has its origins in West Africa and Haiti (*Zumbi*, a snake god; also *sombra*, a Spanish word for *ghost*) but we now use the word *zombie* mostly in three ways:

Definition #1 (best kind of zombie): a soulless corpse that runs around eating people. Used in a sentence: "Run! There are hundreds of zombies sprinting toward us! They are going to eat out our guts! Run!"

Definition #2 (shittier kind of zombie): a person who is apathetic and unresponsive to his or her environment. For example, lots of guys who are in bands act like that. Used in a sentence: "Have you met Chunks? He plays guitar in that noise band from Williamsburg. He's kind of a zombie but he's a really good guitar player. His riffs are very ethereal."

Definition #3 (acceptable): someone who is really tired. Used in a sentence: "I'm so tired. I feel like a zombie. I really need to take a load off."

I am partial to the Type #1 zombie. The Type #1 zombie is truly a free spirit. Unlike me, he is not self-conscious in the least. For example, I think about what I look like to other people whereas the Type #1 zombie has no qualms about going out in public with his clothes tattered, covered in blood, bile, dirt, and *in all likelihood feces*. I envy that kind of self-assuredness. I wouldn't be caught dead out in public with my clothes tattered, bloody, dirty, and in all likelihood covered in feces. (Unless I was dressed up like a zombie for a costume party. Still, that's highly improbable because [a] I don't like parties; and [b] even if I did wear that costume, I wouldn't smear real feces on myself. I might smear fake feces on myself. Likeliest, though, I would smear no feces on myself, fake or otherwise.)

That about sums it up. How the book ends is as much of a mystery to me as it is to you. It's anybody's guess and that's the beauty of creative exploration. In conclusion, the book will be very long, single-spaced, no margins, and the letters will be small. I hope you're as excited about it as I am.

Book Proposal, Part 2

Things I Will Take into Consideration
While Writing the Book

1. "Can This Book Be Made into a Movie?" Should this be simply a profound work of art? Or should this be a profound work of art with box office potential? After much deliberation and, yes, soul-searching, I've concluded that this should be a work of art with box office potential. If a Hollywood development executive gets his/her mitts on the book, here's the pitch: "It's like *Avatar* but very different and much funnier." If you want to know more, then you'll have to keep reading.

2. "Genius Factor" I intend to hire an independent polling company to conduct focus groups among my readers to tabulate the "genius factor." The independent polling company will hand out a questionnaire and sharpened pencils during the focus group sessions. The questionnaire will look like this:

a) "How genius was this book on a scale from 1 to 5?"
b) "On a scale of 1 to 5, how profound was this book?"
c) "In terms of being life-altering, would you say that it was (1) very life-altering, (2) modestly life-altering, (3) garden-variety life-altering, (4) vaguely life-altering, (5) not that life-altering, (6) the opposite of life-altering, (7) none of the above.

3. "Making Sense" Should this book make sense? Should it be cohesive? Should it have a beginning, middle, and end? Should I connect dots? Should I construct a narrative that it is easy and enjoyable for my reader to follow? Or should it be an incoherent mess? I'm still not sure. Gut is telling me that incoherent mess might be my best shot at finishing it.

4. "Can This Book Be Made into an HBO Television Series?" [See #1.]

5. "Should I Hire My Funnier and More Disciplined Friends to Write This Book for Me?" I would pay them of course; probably by the word—not sure what the going rate is, but I'll look into it. Or at least I'll pay someone to look into it for me and then they'll tell me what the "going rate" is and then I'll tell them to invoice me for it and then they'll send me an invoice based off the "going rate" and then I'll pay them.

Book Proposal, Part 3

Things I Won't Take into Consideration
While Writing This Book

1. "Truth" I can't write the memoir I want to write if I stick to the facts. My life simply isn't eventful enough for an accurate portrait. So instead of telling the truth, I will write whatever comes to mind and if I'm asked about it I will just say that memory is subjective. For example: "When I was in high school I spent an entire day with Bigfoot. He was much smarter than I'd expected. Turns out he's, like, this huge jazz buff." Not true—or is it? Maybe it wasn't Bigfoot. Maybe it was this kid Brendan Buckner from chemistry lab. Not sure, memory is subjective.

2. "The Roman Empire" While I can't say that I'm 100 percent sure I won't take the Roman Empire into consideration while writing this book, I can say that I'm at least 80 percent sure.

3. "Meryl Streep's Feelings" There's that saying "Too much of a good thing can be a bad thing."

Book Proposal, Part 4

Everybody Poops Genius Pieces

I want my book to be an "important memoir," okay maybe not as important as *A Heartbreaking Work of Staggering Genius* but, in all likelihood, equally as important, or at the very least, *only slightly less important.*

I want it to be sort of a comic quasi-memoir, from a guy's perspective. Think: *A Heartbreaking Work of Staggering Genius* + *A Million Little Pieces* + *Everything Is Illuminated* + *Oh the Glory of It All* + *Barrel Fever* + *Everybody Poops.* I have a working title: *Oh the Million Little Heartbreaking Pieces of Illuminated Barrel Poops.* Gut tells me this is too long of a title. Here's a few different title options:

- *Everything Is Staggering Little Fever Glory*
- *A Heartbreaking Work of a Million Illuminated Barrels*
- *Everybody Poops Genius Pieces*

Full disclosure: I know that I will never write as good as any of the guys whose books I am trying to do my own version of, but I figure it wouldn't be a bad idea to aim high. For instance: Does a musician pick up a guitar to write a song and be like, "I want to sound just like Jason Mraz?" No of course not. Instead, he thinks to himself, "I want to sound just like Neil Young." And then he *winds up* sounding like Jason Mraz. But he *tried* to sound like Neil Young. Can you fault him? I highly doubt that you could (fault him). In other words, I'm trying to write as well as David Eggers but I sound like Jason Mraz *and that's okay.*

Another title idea for the book is A *Diamond- and Ruby-Encrusted Mind*. This title refers to a serious biological abnormality that I deal with every day of my life; namely, that my mind is encrusted with diamonds and rubies. "That must be a huge drag," you say. Well, not entirely.

The PROS of having a diamond- and ruby-encrusted mind are that *it's a financial nest egg for my children's children*. After I die, they can remove the diamonds and rubies from my mind, have them appraised, and either keep them and let them continue appreciating in value, or, if times are hard, they can sell them at market value and spend the money however they deem most useful. I'm hoping they spend it on college tuition or a home, but it's really their decision.

Another pro is that *it's a good conversation starter*. Whenever there's a lull in conversation—at a dinner party, waiting in line at Starbucks, riding a crowded elevator—I can always blurt out, "Hey, everybody! I have a diamond- and ruby-encrusted mind!" Then they say, "Really?" And I say, "Yes, really. And I have this certificate of authenticity from my neurologist Dr. Opal Finsky and also from Barry Woinsky's Diamond Emporium, 'Meeting All Your Fine Gem Needs Since 1963,' as proof." And then we're off and running, talking a blue streak about this,[5] that,[6] and the other thing.[7]

And of course *I can light my way in the dark*. The diamonds and rubies in my mind store sunlight during the day, and at night, rays of purple light shoot out of my eyeballs. This also provides hours of entertainment for my cats; they like to chase the spots of light as they dart around the room. Sometimes I swing my head around really fast on purpose. They go crazy for that. I get dizzy and oftentimes puke or at very least dry-heave, but it's worth it to see them having so much fun.

Still, in spite of this great stuff, it does have its drawbacks. For example, I get *really bad headaches*. I wouldn't say they're full-blown migraines, but they are pretty bad just the same. Normally, a few aspirin

---

5. "This" would be the weather.
6. "That" would be discovering friends in common.
7. The "other thing" is about whether or not God exists. Between you and me, I say sure.

MY DIAMOND- AND RUBY-ENCRUSTED MIND

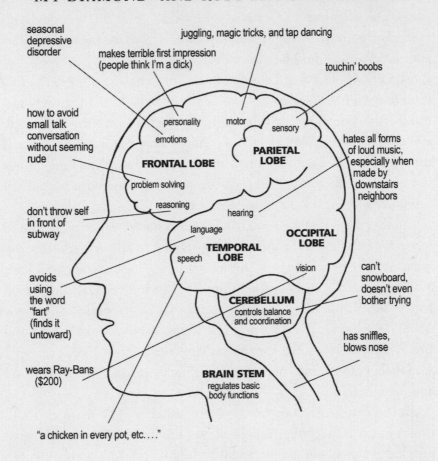

seasonal depressive disorder

juggling, magic tricks, and tap dancing

makes terrible first impression (people think I'm a dick)

touchin' boobs

how to avoid small talk conversation without seeming rude

personality

motor

sensory

emotions

PARIETAL LOBE

FRONTAL LOBE

hates all forms of loud music, especially when made by downstairs neighbors

problem solving

reasoning

don't throw self in front of subway

hearing

language

OCCIPITAL LOBE

TEMPORAL LOBE

speech

vision

avoids using the word "fart" (finds it untoward)

can't snowboard, doesn't even bother trying

CEREBELLUM
controls balance and coordination

has sniffles, blows nose

wears Ray-Bans ($200)

BRAIN STEM
regulates basic body functions

"a chicken in every pot, etc...."

does the trick, but on several occasions, I've actually had to lie down for hours at a time and put a cold pack or a raw T-bone steak on my eyes.

Additionally, *I am a target for cat burglars and jewelry thieves.* Since word has gotten out about the priceless jewels encased inside my skull, I've had no less than five attempted robberies on my cranium. The worst part about this is I have to sleep with a football helmet on. Try sleeping with a football helmet on your head every night and then tell me that you wish you had those diamonds and rubies inside *your* skull. My guess is that you wouldn't be so quick to tell me that. Granted, some chin straps aren't as bad as others, but generally speaking, the chin straps chafe a lot and it's very difficult to ever really get into a nice sleep groove.

And of course the worst part is the *chronic diarrhea*. I can't say for sure that the diarrhea is related to the diamonds and rubies but I have a sneaky feeling it is.

In conclusion: Everybody poops genius pieces, Jason Mraz, Dr. Opal Finsky, chin straps.

Book Proposal, Part 5

A Sack of Moldy Fuckin' Potatoes

I have decided that I will start my book at the end, with a tragic event, and work backwards. I want the reader to wonder, "How did he get there? How did he get to this awful and tragic place?"

It's November of 2002. It's 8 a.m. in the morning.

I am standing on the Brooklyn Bridge. The Eighth Wonder of the World.

I don't know why I am here or how I got here to this awful and tragic place.

Not the bridge, but where I am emotionally is what's tragic and awful.

I'm really hungover. Cuz a all the booze I pounded down through my gullet.

I have barely slept a wink. And what sleep I did was shit.

My head feels like a sack of moldy fuckin' potatoes.

I can still taste last night's mojito in my upchuck. Ya ever had that? Mojito barf?

My mouth tastes like a skunk crawled inside another skunk's butt, and that skunk crawled inside my mouth and took a dump. A dump full of bark and clumps of skunk food.

I got dried-up boot on my Brown University sweatshirt.

I have a really bad stomachache because I ate a meatball parmesan hoagie at four in the morning in a blackout. I got grated parm in my unders.

I wouldn't even have known that if I hadn't woken up with it lying half-
  eaten by my side.
I lie down in the fetal position on a bench. Like a fetal pig.
A couple sitting on the bench moves because I'm touching the woman's
  arm with my sneaker.
Passersby look at me. I can hear them snicker at me.
I wanna jump to m'death.

Important? Yes. Profound? Yes. Able to be made into a movie? Yes. Yes. Yes. (Jake Gyllenhaal would be perfect for the role.) I proofread it twice, then I sent all of the material to Ben.

Several agonizing days later, I heard from Ben about my proposal. He wrote: "Mike, so I really appreciate all the hard work you've done on this. Your proposal and sample chapter was definitely interesting to read, but I wouldn't be doing my job if I didn't tell you that I expected something a little, how should I put this, funnier? Like the part about jumping off the bridge and about how your head felt like a moldy sack of fucking potatoes. Pretty depressing. And why did you say, 'm'death'? Why not just 'my death'? If you're open to it, let's talk about maybe going back to the drawing board on this and rethinking our approach. Honestly, though. It was very interesting. Sincerely, Ben."

Not at all wanting to be "interesting," I immediately wrote Ben back. I said, "Ben, I totally and wholeheartedly agree. Let's switch directions. Best, Sho."

Ben wrote back, "Really? I mean, I don't want to sway you. I can tell that you worked really hard on this. I want you to write what you want to write."

I immediately wrote back, "Nope. Not to worry. I hate everything I wrote. Despise it. It's dead to me. Let's start from scratch."

He wrote back, "Really?"

I wrote back, "Yes. I have already deleted the file."

Getting Started on Writing My Book

Writing a book isn't easy and I knew that if I was going to write a book, then I needed to read one too. In fact, I reckoned I needed to read a bunch of them, all of them, if possible. I wrote down a list of the books that I'd read thus far in my life:

1. *Blubber* by Judy Blume
2. *The Firm* by John Grisham
3. *Superfudge* by Judy Blume
4. *The Pelican Brief* by John Grisham

It was a short list, too short, embarrassingly short. And it only represented the work of two authors: Judy Blume and John Grisham. They were important books and important authors, a solid foundation for sure, but I'd definitely need to read more books if I wanted to have the authority as a writer that I was looking for. I wrote down the names of some books that I'd read part of:

1. *The Sun Also Rises* (first five pages)
2. *A Tale of Two Cities* (a couple of pages)
3. *Anna Karenina* (read some blurbs on the back cover)

For years I'd been saying that I'd like to do more reading, and so I decided to read "The 100 Greatest Novels of All Time." I figured that if I read a book a day I could read the hundred greatest novels of all time in just a shade over three months. Granted, this would set me back a little on my writing, but I figured that it would be worth it. I took out a pen and paper and began to write down the names of what I believed to be "the hundred greatest novels of all time":

1. *The Grape Of Wrath* by John Steinbeck
2. *The Pictures of Dorian Gray* by Author Unknown
3. *Old Yeller* by Author Unknown

These were the books I was supposed to read in middle school. I was running out of ideas, and I had to concede that I wasn't even actually sure if *Old Yeller* was a book. I needed more books for my list, so in my Mind's Eye I pictured myself inside a bookstore. I pictured myself looking around the bookstore. I asked my Mind's Eye, "What books do I see, Mind's Eye?" I started writing down what books I saw in my Mind's Eye. Some titles sprang to mind and I immediately jotted them down:

1. *The History of Salt*
2. *The History of Pepper* (I couldn't be sure if I had even really seen this book)
3. *The History of Salt n' Pepa*

My list was growing. Still, were these the true classics? I googled the words "best + books" and got a few more titles for my list:

1. *War and Peace* by Tolstoy
2. *Portrait of the Artist as a Young Man* by James Joyce
3. *Tender Is the Night* by William Faulkner

I went to the bookstore near my house with my list and a crisp five-dollar bill. I knew that I wouldn't be able to buy all the books on the list but I was eager to make a dent. As it turns out, five bucks hardly even buys you a bookmark in today's economy. My reading experiment had gone bust.

It was a Tuesday afternoon when I made up my mind that I would begin writing the book on Monday morning of the following week. I did so because it was important to me to start fresh and not midweek. Midweek's no good 'cause the cobwebs are starting to form in anticipation of FRIDAY NIGHT!!!

I decided that when Monday morning rolled around, I would rise early, no later than 10:15 a.m., and write all day, maybe longer, maybe I'd pull an all-nighter. I would make myself coffee, a buttered scone—no, not a buttered scone, a bialy! Yes, a bialy! A bialy is like a flat bagel. They're kind of nasty. And I would be showered and dressed. Okay, so I would be showered, dressed, I'd be eating a bialy, and I'd act like a person who has a "process."

Monday arrived and I finally sat down to write. The first draft was due in April of the following year—roughly 365 days. I'd never undergone such a project, but this seemed like more than enough time to write a book. Sitting at my computer, I began to daydream about what it would be like when this first draft was over. I daydreamed that I'd feel "relieved," "spent," and "cautiously optimistic." I imagined that I'd be a guest on the Charlie Rose show. I began to think of what clothes I might buy for the interview: a corduroy blazer with elbow patches; an Irish fisherman's sweater; big boots; a corncob pipe; an old top hat like the one Lincoln wore, or was it a stove pipe... *wait, what's that?... ew... ouch!*

What had just happened? My cat had just licked my nostrils and jogged me out of the daydream about being on Charlie Rose, and I was brought back to the reality that I had yet to generate a single word of text. This was my problem: "I Don't Know How to Write a Book." I washed the smell of turkey and giblets cat food out of my nose and began to strategize.

Engineering backwards from April, I calculated that if I wrote five pages a day, which seemed very doable, I would have an eighteen-hundred-page first draft when the deadline rolled around. Though completely unwritten, I was very impressed by how long my first draft would be. I mean, I highly doubt that Hemingway's books are that long. Although I can't really say for sure because I've never read one. Still,

I'd never written anything longer than a hundred pages, and here I was embarking on an eighteen-hundred-page journey.

I was curious to know what eighteen hundred pages actually looked like, so I went to a nearby Staples Office Supplies store and purchased three reams of paper. When I got home, I unwrapped all the paper and combined it into one stack. Each ream contained five hundred sheets of paper. Using a pencil and pad, I calculated that 3×500 was fifteen hundred pages; I was three hundred pages short.

Upon realizing that I hadn't bought enough paper, I went back to Staples. I went to the paper section, I opened a ream, and I commenced to count out the three hundred additional pieces of paper I needed to buy. At this juncture a bearded man wearing a Staples apron begins to yell at me, "Hey stop that!" and he tells me that I had to purchase the entire ream. "But I don't need an entire ream!" I insisted. "I only need half a ream." He relented, threatened to call security, and so I purchased the entire ream.

Back home, I counted out three hundred sheets of paper and added it to my stack of fifteen hundred sheets. At last, I had reached my goal of assembling a stack of eighteen hundred pieces of paper to see how large my first draft would be once I had written it. Just to be sure that the stack was in fact eighteen hundred pages, I counted each page individually. That took almost all day. Turns out, it was eighteen hundred pages on the nose. (Now you know that when you buy a ream of paper from Staples that says it has five hundred sheets of paper in it, you can believe it!)

I removed one sheet from the stack and placed it in my printer. I turned on my computer, opened a blank document, and wrote the words "Untitled Michael Showalter Novella." I didn't know what a "novella" was or how it differed from a proper "novel," but I'd always liked the sound of it. I have since learned that a "novella" is either a long story or a short novel. Based on this, given the length of my book-to-be, I needed to change the title to "Untitled Michael Showalter *Novel.*"

I printed out my title page and placed it on top of the stack of paper. Then I picked up the stack and carried it into the bathroom so I could see what I looked like holding the manuscript.

I was really impressed by the size of my manuscript. It was really thick and bulky. I must have worked really hard on it. I thought: When I hand this in twelve months from now, my editors will see that this is a manuscript filled with humor, wisdom, sadness, and revelation. And they will be correct. It is impossible to write eighteen hundred pages without plunging and plumbing the depths of the human soul. I was so excited that, at a clip of five pages per day, I had written an eighteen-hundred-page manuscript that plunged and plumbed the depths of the human soul. Then I took a long lunch break: chicken sandwich, chips, Fuji apple.

After lunch I read the *New York Times* and catnapped for two hours. When I awoke, I had a terrible thought: What if eighteen hundred pages is too many pages? If I write an eighteen-hundred-page first draft, will they think I'm a show-off? Or worse, just a crazy person? I mean, at a certain point you're not plunging or plumbing anything, you're just ranting. Any nutjob off the street can write eighteen hundred pages if he's got enough pencils and tablets. They will think that I'm like the Unabomber. Then and there I decided: *I am too prolific for my own good.*

I ran back into my office and peeled a giant portion off the stack. It wasn't quite half the stack, but it was a lot of pages. This shorter draft, around twelve hundred pages, made more sense to me. Twelve hundred pages would be impressive, yes, but not too impressive. Where eighteen hundred pages is like saying, "Hey, look at me, I wrote eighteen hundred pages. Where's my Booker Prize?" twelve hundred pages is like saying, "Look at me, I could have written eighteen hundred pages, but I wrote twelve hundred instead, because I have a lot to say but I don't have to say all of it." Twelve hundred was just the right amount of impressive. I was grateful that I figured that out.

Shortening my first draft from eighteen hundred pages down to twelve hundred pages really gave me a lot of flexibility in terms of planning out how I'd write the book. With the eighteen-hundred-page version, I'd have been writing every day for over a year. Now I only needed to write for 240 days. That gave me roughly 120 days to play with. Who

WRITING SCHEDULE BASED ON 365 DAYS

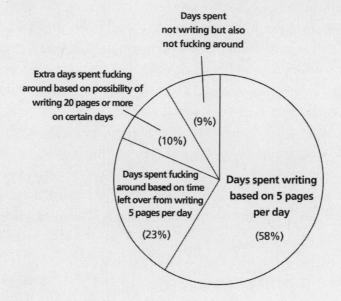

knew writing involved so much math?! There were so many different ways I could schedule my writing:

- I could write for two days, take one day off, then repeat.
- I could write for 240 days straight, and then take three months off to fuck around right before the deadline.
- I could take long weekends.
- I could alternate months.
- I could alternate weeks.

The possibilities seemed overwhelming. How do all my fellow scribes do it? How did Chaucer do it? How did Longfellow do it? Most importantly: Who's Longfellow?[8] Then I had another thought: What if I write ten pages a day instead of five? If I write ten pages a day, then I could finish the book in four months and have eight months to fuck around.

8. Henry Wadsworth Longfellow was an American poet. Strangely enough he was not a long fellow. He was a short fellow, standing at just a shade over two feet tall.

Ten pages seemed like a lot of pages, but I write fast and I don't edit at all. That's my thing: Whatever I write goes in. It's my special rule.

In support of the five-pages-per-day model I also predicted that I'd get on a roll at some point in the writing process and would decide that five pages wasn't enough for one day. Some days I'd write five pages and some days I'd really be inspired and write twenty pages or maybe even fifty pages. I figured that if I stayed with the five-pages-a-day model, then on days when I wrote twenty or more pages, I could divide the pages I'd written that day by ten and then add the result to my 120 days to fuck around. This seemed like the best plan—five pages per day. I decided that my fucking around would begin immediately so I took a donkeynap and fell into a deep, deep sleep. (For more on sleeping, see p. 52.)

Excerpt from My Imaginary Interview with Charlie Rose

INT. CHARLIE ROSE TV SHOW SET—NIGHT

Charlie Rose interviews Michael Showalter against a black backdrop. They both have coffee mugs in front of them. A copy of *Mr. Funny Pants* lies on the table. (Or is it "lays on the table"? Note to self: Ask Ben if it's *lies* or *lays*?) Michael wears a brown tweed coat over a maroon, heavily ribbed turtleneck sweater.

Ed. Note: I think it's lies *but I suggest just cutting the whole section.*
Response to Ed. Note: Thanks, Ben. I will take that into serious consideration.

CHARLIE: Michael, you've been described as "very smart." Do *you* think that you're smart?

MICHAEL: I got good SAT scores, yes. But no. I don't think I'm smart.

CHARLIE: (surprised) Really? You really mean that?

MICHAEL: I really do mean it, Charlie. I've never seen myself that way.

CHARLIE: You're humble.

MICHAEL: Yes, admirably so, heroically so.

CHARLIE: Who do you think is smart?

MICHAEL: Wolf Blitzer seems smart. The way he talks and stuff. His beard.

CHARLIE: What about Albert Einstein?

MICHAEL: What about him?

CHARLIE: Do you think that he's smart?

MICHAEL: I guess so. Supposedly dolphins are and pigs.

CHARLIE: Are what?

MICHAEL: Smart.

CHARLIE: What accounts for your accomplishments?

MICHAEL: Discipline.

CHARLIE: What else?

MICHAEL: Hard work.

CHARLIE: What else?

MICHAEL: Diligence.

CHARLIE: What else?

MICHAEL: I'm out of synonyms for *discipline*, Charlie.

CHARLIE: Dedication?

MICHAEL: That's a good one.

CHARLIE: Where do your ideas come from?

MICHAEL: Where *don't* my ideas come from?

CHARLIE: Tell me.

MICHAEL: Tell you what?

CHARLIE: Where your ideas *don't* come from.

MICHAEL: Uh...trees? Wait, I'm confused.

CHARLIE: You said, "Where *don't* my ideas come from?"

MICHAEL: Right, I guess that was my answer.

CHARLIE: Trees?

MICHAEL: No, I mean technically, yes, I don't get my ideas from trees but I was more just saying that I get ideas from everywhere. It's less about where I don't get them. Forget it.

CHARLIE: What drives you?

MICHAEL: (thinks, then) A car.

CHARLIE: What else?

MICHAEL: A taxi, a subway; once for a wedding, a stretch limo. Where is this going?

CHARLIE: What else?

MICHAEL: What is this, Charlie? The fucking Spanish Inquisition? How many questions are you going to ask me?

CHARLIE: It's an interview, Mike.

MICHAEL: That's *Michael* to you, Mr. Rose!

CHARLIE: I'm just trying to do my job!

MICHAEL: And I'm just telling you to mellow your flabby ass out!

CHARLIE: Maybe we should wrap it up?

MICHAEL: I think that would be best. Don't you?

CHARLIE: I...I...I...

MICHAEL: Well, maybe this will clear things up, Charlie. (Michael takes off his mic.)

MICHAEL: This interview is over!

CHARLIE: But—

MICHAEL: IT'S OVER, CHARLIE! Don't you get it? It's OVER! It's over and you blew the interview by asking me so many questions!

CHARLIE: But—

MICHAEL: Christ, Charlie! Drop it! Okay?! Just...ACH!!! (Michael punches Charlie in the ribs and storms off set.)

CHARLIE: Ow! That really hurt.

THE END

Duck Imprinting

Long before I knew what being a "Democrat" meant, I was a Democrat, for the sole reason that my parents were Democrats. I never questioned it. I'm sure that if my parents were Republicans I'd be a Republican and I'd be writing a different book right now. Also true, I believe that if ducks raised me I'd think I was a duck. Luckily, ducks didn't raise me because I don't like traveling much and ducks seem to migrate a lot. Conversely, if I raised a duck, the duck would think that he or she was human. This is called *imprinting*.

I don't want to get too into the "imprinting" of ducks but in a nutshell: When baby ducks, or ducklings, are born, they believe that they are the *same species* as whatever living creature they see first upon entering the world, and they will, to the best of their ability, mimic the behavior of that being. This process is known as "imprinting." But I really don't want to get too into it, so I'll just add that if a duck saw Wolf Blitzer first, he'd probably try to get into the news business. I doubt he'd succeed because of his limitations (inability to talk, read, write, think) but he'd try. Anyway, I don't want to get into a whole long thing about duck imprinting.

But, yes, for what it's worth, if the duck saw a weasel or a bear, the duck would think that it too was a weasel or a bear. But as we all know, unfortunately for the duck, at some point, the weasel or the bear would eat it, but that's beside the point. The duck would still think it was a weasel or a bear. (Apropos of nothing, if the weasel and the bear mated we'd call it a *beasel* or a *wear*.)

BUT NOT DOGS!

Ducks and dogs are different in this way because a dog will always know that it's a dog. Even a socialized dog that has been whispered to by the Dog Whisperer knows he's a dog. The dog could read and write and throw cocktail parties for graduate students and listen to bad indie rock—he would still know he's a dog! Not so with ducks because even if a few weeks later they see another duck, they will still think that they are Wolf Blitzer (or a "beasel") and not ducks. They might recognize the other duck as a "sibling" (even if it's their actual mother) but they still consider the human to be their "mother" and this is true even if the human they saw first was a man (example: Wolf Blitzer).

In conclusion: I am a product of my parents and the choices that they made for me before I was able to make choices for myself. If they were ducks or Republicans I wouldn't be writing this book. If I were a Republican I'd be writing a different book, and if I were a duck I'd be migrating south, floating on a pond, or eating "smallest fishes."

AN EXCERPT OF THE BOOK THAT I'D BE WRITING IF I WERE A REPUBLICAN
(For non-Republican version, go back to "Introduction.")

One morning, while checking my email on my IBM commuter, listening to "Get My Drink On" by Toby Keith on constant repeat, sipping a mug of grande decaf mocha caramel spice with three lumps of sugar, tons of cinnamon powder, and extra foam, and reading up on the latest news regarding the upcoming presidential election between war hero, statesman, and all-around good guy John McCain and some sketchy Nubian from Chicago, I received an email from Ben Greenberg, a Jewishy-sounding book editor from New York City (aka Europe). He mentioned as a way of breaking the ice that he'd read my essay "If You

Don't Like It Here in the U.S. of A. Then Get the Fuck Out!" and asked if I had any interest in writing a book. This raised my hackles.[9]

THE MAN FROM THE BEAUTIFUL FOREST

All "important memoirs" start with a section where the author tells his reader "where I came from." (I mean, they tell you where *they* came from. They don't tell you where *I* came from! Can you imagine if that guy who wrote *Angela's Ashes* had started his book with a story about where *I* was from? That would be really weird but also very cool.)

Europe in the Fifteenth Century: It all started for me on the eastern borders of Switzerland in the port principality of Lichtenstein. Lichtenstein has been around since the Middle Ages. The Middle Ages was back when everyone ran around in "pelts" (I think) and when the Vikings were scuffling around ransacking and pillaging things, eating mutton and big turkey legs, and drinking grog. It was also when ugg boots were invented and the Rolling Stones made their first album. Other "Ages" are:

The Stone Ages: This was when everyone was into using stones as tools because they were too stupid to use anything else. No offense to people from the Stone Ages but it's true. They were stupid.

The Iron Ages: This was when they were smart enough to use iron but not much else. For instance, people during the Iron Ages would have no use for an electric toothbrush because they'd have nothing to plug it into. Technically, I suppose if it came precharged, then they'd be able to use it until the battery ran out, but once the battery expired they'd have no way to recharge it. (To say nothing of the fact that Crest toothpaste

9. A hackle is a long, slender feather on the neck of a male goose. I'm not a goose. I hunt geese. Don't get me wrong. I hunt them down and kill them. I'm just not one myself.

didn't exist either and don't even think about Tom's brand toothpaste. Don't even think about that.)

The Dark Ages: This was in between the fall of the Roman Empire and the Middle Ages. The Dark Ages lasted from AD 500–1500. During those thousand years it was dark all the time. That's why they called it the Dark Ages—no light whatsoever. The sun wasn't working. It set one sunny Monday in AD 500 and didn't rise again for a thousand years. Inexplicably, it had flickered out and no one could figure out how to flicker it back on—the use of candles, flashlights, and glow sticks nearly quadrupled during this time. This was when the first techno-rave was documented (tavern in Persia, AD 800). One Tuesday in AD 1500, a Moravian spice merchant named Brad realized that the bulb inside the sun just wasn't fully screwed in, so they screwed it back in and it flickered on again. Brad went back to selling his spices.

The Bronze Ages: This came some time after the Dark Ages when the sun flickered back on. This was when people got tan like crazy. The skin of kings, queens, and serfs alike was all a beautiful copper bronze. If you didn't have a good tan, you couldn't sell any goods at the market. No one would barter with you for goods at the market if your tan was shitty. Worse even were those sorry few who burned easily. The bronzed elite called them Crab People and they were regularly beheaded in the center of town very near the market where everyone was selling goods.

The Ice Ages: This is a Disney animated movie with Ray Romano and Cedric the Entertainer doing voices. (How amazing is it that Cedric's last name is "the Entertainer," considering he went on to become an entertainer? Lucky for him he chose that profession. Like, if he'd tried to be a doctor or something everyone would say, "Come on, Cedric, entertain us," and then he'd have to say, "No, it's just my last name.")

Back to Lichtenstein: There's a small town in Lichtenstein called Schaan, which is surrounded by the Schaanwald or "Beautiful Forest." Legend says that early in the 1400s a man came from this forest and was known to his neighbors as the Schaanderwalder or "man from the Beautiful Forest." In time the name became Schowalder and then in America, many years later, Showalter. In other words, I am "Michael the Man from the Beautiful Forest." This is kind of absurd if you know me because I really hate camping.

- My clothes always smell like campfire, bark, and bug spray.
- I prefer "firm queen-size bed" to "lumpy, moldy sleeping bag."
- I don't like "powdered" food.
- Mosquitoes seem to have a love affair with my blood.
- Identifying different types of spores is interesting for only a short amount of time.
- Ghost stories make me scared of homicidal maniacs lurking outside my tent.
- I like to watch a little TV or DVR before bed.
- Hiking is fun but only if there's a lodge with a Jacuzzi involved at some point.
- My version of "roughing it" is not having an electric toothbrush.
- I always get poison ivy in the worst places like on my dick or in my butt crack.

Cut to: 560 years later. My dad was a young professor in the French department at Haverford College, and my mom was an undergraduate English major at Bryn Mawr College. They met while helping to remodel an old church into a coffee shop where young people of every race could congregate. It was a place for folk music, spirited political debate, poetry readings, and, I'm guessing, some serious pot huffing.

My mother is descended from Ukrainian Jews who came to America in the early 1900s. She grew up in the Boston suburb of Brookline and wanted to be a professional whistler. She is a very good whistler but chose to be an academic instead. Like my mother, I am also a good whistler. I can whistle "Eleanor Rigby" in four-part harmony.

My father is Episcopalian. His ancestors emerged from the beautiful forest and eventually came to America in the 1600s. He is a distant relative of James Madison. James Madison is one of our country's founding fathers, and the fourth president of the United States of America. I know you're probably already making this connection but, yes, that means I'm also related to James Madison's wife, Dolly Madison, who, I'm pretty certain, invented ice cream.

I like to imagine what life must have been like back in the 1700s. One thing is for sure—everyone was really dirty. I mean, I guess no one has time for bathing when you're fighting a big revolution for "free will" or whatever. Either way, I can't help but think that everyone must have had really bad B.O. in the 1700s. I think that's why they wore so much perfume—to drown out how much they all smelled like burritos. I'd be all like, "Yo, Ben Franklin! You've got some seriously stanky B.O. wafting over in my general direction. I mean, I know you helped write the Declaration of Independence and whatnot but you need some Old Spice, because you stink like a burrito!" Now I'm wondering if they even had burritos back in the 1700s. Probably not.

UPDATE: I just ~~went to the New York Public Library~~ googled "Burrito + 1700s." What came up was an article about how the sandwich was "invented" in the 1700s by the fourth Earl of Sandwich (legend has it that he ordered some meat "tucked" between two pieces of bread). I also found out that more recently a Massachusetts court ruled that burritos *weren't* sandwiches. The judge determined that in order for something to be a "true sandwich" two pieces of bread must be involved. Massachusetts is known to be very strict about sandwich legislation. (Iowa and Vermont have much less stringent sandwich bylaws.)

I wonder who the third Earl of Sandwich was? Gonna google right now. Hold on. Okay, his name was Edward Montagu. He was just kind of a douchey rich kid. He didn't invent anything. Shit, OCD is making me have to look up the first and second Earls of Sandwich too. Okay, first Earl of Sandwich was also named Edward. He died at sea. Second Earl of Sandwich married a woman named Lady Ann Boyle who was the daughter of the second Earl of Cork. FUCK! Gotta look up Earl of Cork now. Okay, just looked up Earl of Cork. He was Irish and was accused of treason at some point. Shit. I've completely lost my train of thought.

Part One

Early Memories

Today I wrote a few little reviews of "my book that I haven't written yet" and I posted them above my desk. They are just snippets of longer reviews. The reviews that I wrote of my own book that hasn't been written yet say things like:

"Generational masterpiece"
"Transcendent work of quasi-semi-non-fiction"
"Profound, somewhat vaguely true story"
"Sheds light on the human condition"

I even wrote a middling review just to stay humble. It read, "Spotty prose."

These reviews that I wrote of "my book that I haven't written yet" give me something to aspire to. I will write a memoir that will be impossible for readers to put down. It will be profound, funny, and deeply meaningful.

With great vigor, I have started to write and I have begun with my first memory ever. This memory will illustrate the comic trope that comedy = tragedy + time. (For more on comedic tropes, see "The Rule of Threes," p. 91.)

I'm four years old. I'm in my living room. I'm roughhousing with my uncle. I karate kick him in the balls and he topples over in agony. I laugh. He groans. Now my parents are running into the living room to help my uncle. He gets up and they all go into the kitchen. My relationship with my uncle never recovered from that moment. He sort of ignored me forever. Like, have you ever played with a really adorable puppy and then it farts, or rubs its boner on you, and you never want to go near it again for the rest of your life? That about sums up my childhood: a smelly puppy, with a boner.

Today I wrote out no less than twelve different versions of the above paragraph. I just keep writing it, over and over again, in a million different ways and styles, trying to get it "perfect."

MY FIRST MEMORY EVER—IN THE STYLE OF WILLIAM SHAKESPEARE

I hadst walketh the earth for nary four annum when I didst encounter mine father's dear kinsman. Kicketheth him in the loins, I didst. A cheery guffaw didst escape my lips. But didst mine kinsman speak in like manner? Nay, he did not! In agony, like a beast pierced with bow and javelin, or like a lover thusly scorned, he didst wail.

MY FIRST MEMORY EVER—IN THE STYLE OF WILLIAM CARLOS WILLIAMS

so much depends
upon
a puppy's boner
stiff and red
rubbing against
your legs.

Am I just chasing my own tail here? What's "perfect"? And when will I know? The truth of the matter is that I keep working on this memory because I genuinely do not know what to write next. Then it dawned on me. How can my life story be interesting to other people if it isn't even interesting to me? I can't make an entire book out of one memory where I kicked my uncle in the balls. But then I thought, "Or can I?" It was an "Aha!" moment. Maybe I can! That would be unique, a whole book mining one memory. Then I came crashing down to reality. It's ridiculous. I'll need more. I need more memories, more subject matter. After several attempts at the uncle balls story, I moved on to another formative memory.

After first grade, my parents go on leave from teaching, and we move to London for a year. "On leave" is fancy college speak for "paid vacation." We live in a small "flat"; we eat "crisps" and "biscuits" and drink "pop." "Flat" means apartment; "crisps" means potato chips; "biscuits" means cookies; and "pop" means… pop. I wear "plimsoles." That's what they call sneakers in the UK. More specifically, plimsoles are rubber-soled cloth shoes.

Ed. Note: Hey, Mike, I'm feeling like the glossary of British words is really sort of just instructional and not necessary in the least.

We go to see a production of William Shakespeare's Taming of the Shrew *at the National Theatre. Before the play starts, a drunk guy creates a disturbance in the theater. The ushers have to subdue him and drag him out of the building. Everyone in the audience is very upset and agitated. My sister starts crying. I'm loving it. It is unexpected and surprising. I also have a gut feeling that it's a joke. When the curtain rises again and the play begins, the drunk guy turns out to be the main character, Petruchio, "a brash young man from Verona." It is a joke! This is an aha moment for me. I have some vague thought that I might like to do something like this one day.*

As I finish writing this memory, I hear a voice in my head. It is a loud voice, clear and articulate—the voice of God. The voice says, "Hey,

Showalter, no one cares about Petruchio or your stupid story about William Shakespeare. Make poop jokes!"

We return from London to New Jersey in 1977, and I begin third grade. I notice right away that I am a little bit different from my classmates. I speak with a British accent. I call my mom Mummy, which the other kids find quite bizarre. I also wear brown plimsoles. This is social suicide. Brown sneakers are all the rage in the UK but in America in 1977, kids wear blue sneakers. Wearing brown sneakers is like wearing dog poop on your feet and the other kids let me know this. They say things like:

"Hey dog poop feet!" or . . .

"Hey poop shoes!" or . . .

"Hey, Showalter, you've got dog shit for feet!"

I beg my mom to buy me some blue sneakers so that I will fit in with my classmates. She takes me to JCPenney and buys me a shiny pair of blue sneakers with four stripes. It turns out that four stripes are even worse than brown sneakers. I need to have three stripes. You'd think that four stripes would be one stripe cooler than three stripes, but it's actually the polar opposite: Four stripes are FOUR STRIPES lamer than three stripes. I beg my mom to buy me some blue sneakers with three stripes instead of four. She refuses.

Even Gangbangers Get the Sniffles

I tried to write this morning but I couldn't focus because I didn't get any sleep last night. If I don't get enough sleep, then I will catch a cold and nothing is worse for me than catching a cold. When I get colds I get the sniffling, sneezing, stuffy head, fever, so I can't rest kind of cold. I am a walking snot machine. Though in a certain sense I do think that colds are kind of cute. Like this one time I was on a subway and I saw a gangbanger sitting across from me on the subway car. I knew he was a gangbanger because he had a tattoo of a teardrop under his eye. I think that means he's killed someone in prison with a shiv.

So I'm looking at him. And he's just gazing out the window of the subway and he doesn't know I'm watching him. I'm looking at him and I'm thinking, "I hope he doesn't see me looking at him because if he does he might pop a cap in me," and then suddenly he takes out a Kleenex and blows his nose. Do you see how amazing that is? *He had the sniffles!* This was a huge revelation to me. Even gangbangers get the sniffles. He was so cute.

I feel like blowing your nose is just a really basic human behavior. Like no matter how tough you are, it's cute. Another thing like that is watching someone eating food alone who doesn't know they're being watched. Like they are just sitting there with their little sandwich eating away, their minds totally blank, chewing on their little sandwiches with totally blank expressions on their faces, like little birds eating seeds. I think that if I saw a gangbanger eating a sandwich alone, I'd probably think that he was like a cute little bird eating seeds. I mean, I'd never tell him that because he might pop a cap in me, but I'd be thinking it for sure.

Often I don't get much sleep because I live on a noisy street in Brooklyn, New York. Sometimes there's construction on the street and what's really great for me is that the construction usually starts around midnight and ends around five o'clock in the morning. By "really great for me" I actually mean "really not great for me" because there's nothing I hate more than the sounds of cranes, jackhammers, and metal hitting metal outside my window all night long while I try to sleep. Sometimes I swear I can actually hear the foreman telling his guys, "Okay, fellows! Let's make some noise! Hit that metal against that metal harder!"

On one such night, my girlfriend suggested that I take a mild anxiety pill to help me sleep. I was reluctant to take the pill because, frequently, sleeping aids can be addictive, and I have an addictive personality, so I'm hesitant to take them but she told me that I had nothing to worry about. She said that it was basically a vitamin, like Saint-John's-Wort. And so I'm like, "Who is Saint John? Like I want to eat some fucking old dude's wart." She said it was basically just a "chill out" pill and that I probably wouldn't even notice it.

Cut to: I take the pill and I'm peeing, not peeing while taking the pill, later I'm peeing. After taking the pill is when I'm peeing is what I'm trying to say. Anyway, as I'm peeing I feel the need to fall unconscious sweeping over me faster than I can push the urine out of my wiener into the toilet bowl. Now I am faced with a major dilemma. Do I finish peeing and risk collapsing on the floor of my bathroom? Or do I try to make it back to my bed before I pass out?

Cut to: I'm stumbling through my apartment toward my bedroom with pee dribbling down my thigh.

Cut to: My next memory is of waking up the next day. Everything else is blackness. I felt as though my head weighed a thousand pounds. It wasn't so much a hangover as it was the sensation of having had a down comforter or a pound cake stuffed inside my brain, or maybe the way it would feel if a moose sat on your head. It was sort of that feeling you get when you wake up from a nap—disoriented.

Like I could take a nap at 4:15 p.m. and then I'll wake up twenty minutes later and have absolutely no clue where I am. I'm like, "What era is this? Is it the 1920s? Am I a flapper? Should I go and put on a flapper costume and go flap at a party?" Then I'm like, "Is that what flappers even do? Flap? Is *flapping* a verb?" I'm that out of it. And I'm also drenched in sweat. Like some little Dutch boy in knickers ran over to me while I was sleeping and poured a bucket of water on me. Or like I have malaria and it's 1932 and I'm surrounded by mosquito netting. I'm drenched. I'm covered in goo. I'm like a baby deer covered in placenta hobbling around trying to learn how to walk, thinking that it's the 1920s and I'm a flapper and there's a little Dutch boy running around with a bucket of water. That's what naps are like for me.

So I call my girlfriend and ask her what this pill was because it clearly wasn't just a "chill pill." She says, "It's called Seroquel." So I look up Seroquel on Google. *I find out that it's a pill that they give to schizophrenics.* It's a pill they give to schizophrenics who are freaking out! It's a pill that they give to naked, bearded dudes, covered in scratches, who are running around in a creek claiming to be Jesus Christ. It's not a pill they give to a mildly annoyed Brooklyn comedian trying to grab a little shut-eye. It's an antipsychotic! So I research further. Besides schizophrenia here are some of the other things that Seroquel is used for:

Post-Traumatic Stress Syndrome: As in, a drug for people who have fought in wars.
Acute Mania: This is very different from Beatlemania. Acute mania is like that scene in *Close Encounters* where Richard Dreyfuss makes the mountain out of the mashed potatoes and his son starts to cry.

Side effects of Seroquel include mild weight gain or... mild weight loss. In other words, they have no fucking clue what will happen to your body when you take it. They're just covering their tracks: "You might get fat, you might get skinny, we're really not sure."

Another side effect of Seroquel that I found suspicious was "increased paranoia." I thought it treated schizophrenia? Basically, it makes you *more* schizophrenic.

The next one truly boggled my mind. Seroquel treats *autism*. I took a pill that *treats* autism. I actually didn't realize that you could treat autism. Like what? If you're autistic and you take Seroquel suddenly you can communicate and form relationships?

My father told me that he thinks he has Asperger's Syndrome, which is a mild form of autism. It's pronounced "ass burgers." Asperger's is essentially a disease of social awkwardness. Can you imagine a name for a disease of social awkwardness any worse than Asperger's? If you're already socially awkward nothing would exacerbate that more than to have to explain your social awkwardness by saying that you have "Ass Burgers." That's not going to alienate you from people at all. "What's wrong with Jim?" "He has ass burgers!" "Hahahahahaha." It's a self-perpetuating disease name. Having to say you have ass burgers only makes you more socially awkward! They should call it Supercoolberger's Syndrome and then people would be more confident and become less awkward.

My favorite new disease is Restless Leg Syndrome. There is a drug for it called Requip. Side effects of Requip include: nausea, dizziness, and vomiting. I'd never heard of this ailment before so I went online and researched it more. Apparently, it's got lots of different names including: Jiggly Legs, Jimmy Jams, "The Kicks," and Sewing Machine Foot. You can understand why they made it sound more ominous and called it Restless Leg Syndrome. Putting *syndrome* at the end makes it scary. Jiggly Legs sounds kinda fun.

The main symptom of Restless Leg Syndrome is "the urge to move." By this definition, I'd say most of humanity probably needs Requip. I also read that some sufferers of Restless Leg Syndrome find relief after "drinking a glass of water." In other words, you can either drink a glass of water or pay a lot of money for a drug that makes you puke and shit in your pants.

I saw an anti-steroids ad recently that struck me as odd. In the commercial, we see on a table a tennis ball, a basketball, and a football. The voice-over says in an imposing voice that all of our organs will shrink if we take steroids: kidneys, liver, heart. With each bad thing he mentions, one of the balls deflates. Then at the end he says, "These aren't the only things that will shrink if you take steroids!" And then the last ball deflates. In other words, he's saying that our balls and our penises will shrink. I'm thinking, why make it into a brainteaser? Why not just say, "If you take steroids, your penis will shrink"? That's way worse than organ failure. No guy gives a crap about his kidneys, but tell him that his dick will shrink and he won't go anywhere near steroids.

In fact, I think that they could say that about all things that are really bad for you, whether it's true or not, and guys wouldn't do them. "Smoking will make your penis smaller!" "Sugar shrinks your dick!" And you could use reverse psychology for women. "Smoking will make you grow a penis!" It's probably not true but it's very effective propaganda.

Lots of medical problems have bad names that only make the disease sound worse. Like *hemorrhoids* or *diarrhea*. Those are such gross words. *Athlete's foot* is a good name for a disease because it's something you can be kind of proud of. "I'm an athlete! I play sports! I have feet! Give me powder!" I think that all diseases should have nice names like that. For example: Gonorrhea. They should call it Fucker's Cock. That's a name you can brag about. "I have Fucker's Cock from so much fuckin'! Gimme powder!" Or *dandruff.* It's such an unpleasant word, why not call it *sparkles*? *Sparkles* is a cute word. "Hi, I have sparkles. Do you have any shampoo for my sparkles?"

Mix Tapes

My girlfriend recently asked me to make her a mix tape. I've been worrying about it all week. Mix tapes are problematic for me because there's so much pressure to impress her with my *eclectic* musical interests. My problem is that I don't actually have eclectic musical interests. I like Journey and Sting's solo stuff. She absolutely hates Sting's solo stuff. She doesn't even know half of what I really listen to because I'm ashamed to admit that I like it so I hide it in my iPod under different names. Like, Journey is hidden under Sufjan Stevens and Sting's solo stuff is hidden under Clap Your Hands Say Yeah. I want her to think I'm cool. I'll probably never give it to her but here's the tape so far:

TRACK 1: "CRASH INTO ME" BY THE DAVE MATTHEWS BAND

I mean, can't we just admit at this point that his slow jams are fucking great? And I don't care that he's from South Africa. I know he was against apartheid and I know that because he has black dudes in his band. Whenever I hear this song I wanna put on a white baseball cap, turn it backwards, grab a plastic cup, buy a keg, get one of those Lance Armstrong bracelets that say "Meditate," shave my chest, drench my body in Axe, wear a shark tooth necklace on a leather strap, get a band of thorns tattooed around my upper arm, slap on a cock ring, date-rape my girlfriend, dye the tips of my hair blond, turn my necktie into a belt, vote for Bush, bash fags, and eat Gainers Fuel.

TRACK 2: "ALL I WANNA DO" BY SHERYL CROW

I have Sheryl Crow hidden in my iPod under Cat Power. Friends will be looking through my iPod and be like, "You like Cat Power?" And I'm like, "Are you kidding me? I love Cat Power. I have all their shit." I'm not realizing that Cat Power is one person. And then they're like, "Really? What's your favorite Cat Power song?" And then I'm like, "I know, right?" And then I say, "Look over there! It's a baby deer!" And then when they turn to look I run away.

It's like, do you ever go to Denny's and you're so excited because you order something and it comes to you looking EXACTLY the way it did on the menu? That's what this song is to me. Except it's not a Grand Slam breakfast. It's a Sheryl Crow song. And who cares that an hour later you take a weird shit like you ate a dead bird? It's a great song.

TRACK 3: "BEAUTIFUL" BY CHRISTINA AGUILERA

When I hear this song I feel like I know what it's like to be a teenage girl, you know? Christina is singing directly to me. She knows what makes me happy and what makes me sad. She knows my fears, my joys, my angers, my confusions. And before I know it I'm journaling at a feverish pace. I'm binging and purging and cutting. I'm cutting because I want to feel something! That's why I cut! To feel! Because I'm so fucking numb half the time! And my Dad is such a dick! He doesn't understand me at all. But Christina understands completely!

TRACK 4: "DROPS OF JUPITER" BY TRAIN

I am telling you to your face that I love this song. I—love—it. I sing it all the time. I sing my own complicated harmonies to the chorus. I rewind my favorite parts. When I take road trips I blast it out the window. I own the record. I bought it with real money. I think the lyrics are awesome. "Tell me! Did you sail across the sun? Did you make it to the Milky Way to see the lights all faded? And that Heaven is overrated!" And it's so true. Heaven really is overrated! You know? Heaven gets *way too much* credit in our society and "Drops of Jupiter" points that out. You know, I might just be a lonely passenger here on planet Earth but this is one Train I hope never leaves the station. Especially if it's going to a concentration camp and I'm on the train. I want to stay on the train until the war ends.

TRACK 5: "HIGHER" BY CREED

Catch me alone in my home listening to this song and you will find a grown man in his underwear air guitaring in front of a hundred thousand imaginary screaming Christian rock fans. Scott Stapp sounds like he has a dry donut in his mouth when he sings. You know? It's like a cinnamon powdered Entenmann's donut. But who cares?!! This song rocks! It's has great power chords! It's got a positive message! It makes me want to dick slap God! Kudos, Creed!

Important Addendum

I went on Google and discovered this copy of Creed's backstage rider agreement, which I believe corroborates my observation.

CREED BACKSTAGE RIDER

8 Clean white towels
1 Box cinnamon powdered donuts for Scott
1 Cheese and fruit plate
1 Case domestic beer

Dream Jokes

Probably my biggest fear in writing this book is that I will get "writer's block." Writer's block is what happens when a writer is so freaked out by his own insignificance as a writer that he can't write. It's when he realizes that he won't ever write as well as he wishes that he could. It's the writer's version of stage fright, or the adult film star's version of erectile dysfunction. In order to avoid this (writer's block not erectile dysfunction), I have purchased several how-to books on unlocking one's creativity. For example, I have begun to keep a "Dream Journal" to help me "tap into" my creativity. Every morning I wake up and I write down my dreams.

> *Dear Dream Journal,*
> *Last night I dreamt that I was in a theater seeing a play. I needed to go to the bathroom. The usher pointed me to aisle J. I could see that the toilet was just another seat in the theater, in between two people watching the play. I had to ask everyone to get up so that I could sit on the toilet. I was sitting on the toilet, trying to poop, in the middle of a crowded theater aisle with a play being performed on the stage in front of me. It was a bit embarrassing because I was drawing attention away from the play and toward myself.*

I used to have a recurring anxiety dream that it's the first day of school and I've forgotten to wear a shirt. It's autumn and all the other kids are wearing sweaters and jackets. I'm topless and cold. In the dream, I think to myself, "How could I have possibly forgotten to wear a shirt?" I spend the entire rest of the day trying to find a shirt but I can't find one. In the dream I feel horrified. I don't want my classmates to see me naked. I don't want them to see my true self. I have nowhere to hide. I am exposed. It's the "Naked in Public" dream. My extreme discomfort in the dream suggests that I don't want to, or am afraid to, let my class-mates to see the real me.

I wonder what Matthew McConaughey's dreams are like? Does he dream that it's the first day of school and he *is* wearing a shirt? In the dream, does he think, "How could I possibly have forgotten to take this shirt off?"

Lately, I've been dreaming jokes. In the dream, I think that it's the funniest joke in the world. In the morning when I wake up and I write the joke down, I realize that it doesn't make as much sense because dreams have their own logic. For example:

Q: How many prison guards does it take to screw in a lightbulb?
A: Two. Ethan Murphy and Lieutenant John Chapman.

It's a dream joke. It has its own logic.

Q: Why are there five players on a hockey team?
A: Because six is an even number and four is *also* an even number.

Q: What do you get when you cross a Boy Scout and a sled dog?
A: A "firedog."

Q: What has two thousand legs and is three tables long?
A: A prom wedding.

Q: Why do birds migrate south?
A: Because if they didn't they'd end up just like Lars—a total loser.

They're dream jokes. They have their own logic.

DREAM I HAD OF GOING TO THE
BATHROOM IN A THEATER

My Morning Routine

In order to release my creativity, in addition to my "Dream Journal" I have also begun a "Morning Joke Journal." Every morning I write down at least five jokes—I don't censor.

1. By the time Napoleon was thirty-four years old he had conquered most of Europe. By the time I was thirty-four years old I had conquered most of the Sunday *Times* crossword puzzle that I had started working on two weeks before my thirty-fourth birthday.

2. I like to get adages wrong but still keep the meaning. Instead of saying "You're working at such a snail's pace," I might say "You're working at such a snail's *rate*."

3. I hate that thing they put on DVDs that reads, "The picture on your screen has been modified from its original version. It has been formatted to fit your screen." It's so confusing to me. It should read, "The picture on your screen has been modified IN THAT it has been formatted to fit your screen." I mean, without them saying "in that," how am I supposed to know *in what way* it's been modified? "The picture on your screen has been modified. It has been formatted to fit your screen." But how has it been modified?! Am I just supposed to ASSUME that the two sentences are related to each other?

4. I was in a bagel store the other day and someone ordered an "everything" bagel. The person behind the counter said, "We're out of

everything, but we have everything else." I thought that was kind of a profound statement.

5. I was puttering around my house the other day and I had a soccer match on the TV but I wasn't watching it. I was just listening and I heard the announcer say, "Anything you do that allows balls to be driven into your box will hurt you." I thought to myself, "That has nothing whatsoever to do with soccer but I can only assume, from a woman's perspective, that he's right about it."

Beat Poetry

In high school, I began listening to Bob Dylan and Charles Mingus. I grew my hair a little shaggy and started wearing a jeans jacket and small leather boots. I read "Howl" by Allen Ginsberg and *Dharma Bums* by Jack Kerouac. "On the Road" was too obvious. Only poseurs read "On the Road." I was no poseur. I was the real deal. I read poems: "A Coney Island of the Mind" by Lawrence Ferlinghetti and "Bomb" by Gregory Corso. I was hip to their vibe. They were cool cat daddios and so was I. They were counterculture and so was I. They liked jazz and so did I. They were artists and poets and so was I. We were all bound together by a thread of oneness that...bound us together...in a thread...of... um...oneness.

My senior year, I became the editor-in-chief of my high school's literary magazine: *The Cheshire Cat*. The job had been passed down through the years from cool-arty-graduating-senior to cool-arty-incoming-senior. A guy named John was the editor before me. He was mysterious and deep. He wore a necklace made of seashells, and button-down shirts unbuttoned to his navel.

As editor in chief, I took my role very seriously. I solicited poetry and short stories from my classmates and selected which submissions would be published. I retyped all the pieces on my mom's electric typewriter and spent hours assembling the pages into a pamphlet: I cut, I collated, I stacked. I wrote the following introduction:

INTRODUCTION

A youthful voice can be eloquent, musical, impassioned, and gracious. Yet it can also be coarse, angry, vulgar, and acrimonious.

"Acrimonious"? I must have been studying for the SATs.

But whatever sounds emerge from young voices, they should not be dismissed as uncultured, unknowing, or immature. The work of a writer or artist in development can be just as meaningful as that of a professional, sometimes even more so, and this work should be heard.

"Sometimes even more so"!

These voices, however, are many times stifled by those who are trying to carve a writer to their specifications and not let the vitality that is inherent in the works come through. We believe that these voices should be heard regardless of their content and in the exact form that they are presented to us.

I don't know to whom I am referring when I say "we," like I had an entire staff of people working under me. The "we" was just me.

Arnold Epstein in Neil Simon's *Biloxi Blues* said, "Don't you know that if you compromise your thoughts, you can't be a writer?" We advocate this philosophy and acknowledge all writers, no matter how beautiful, humorous, caustic, morbid, lusty, or dull their works are.

Wow, there's a lot going on there. First of all, how about that quote? Could I not think of anyone cooler to quote than Arnold Epstein? Also, I slipped in two more SAT words: *caustic* and *morbid.* How about "lusty"? I was still a virgin then. I hadn't even masturbated.

**This year's *Cat* is a powerful combination of poetry, politics
and prose.**

Now it's just "*Cat*." I'm clearly saying that there's really no need to use
the whole title now. *The Cheshire Cat* is so well-known I can refer to it
by its nickname.

**In this *Cat* we have tried to represent the poems in a generic
and simple graphic set. We have done this in emulation of the
great poetry journals published by the Beats in the late 1950s.**

Again, there was no "we." It was just "me." Then this thing: "Graphic
set"? I can only assume I couldn't think of a better word than *set*.

**We had to read each piece at least twice before the quality and
meaning hit us.**

"At least twice," he says. What dedication! Most editors wouldn't do
that. Most editors probably barely even read what they put in their magazines at all, but not me. I read each piece twice.

We strongly recommend that you do the same.

Now I'm just being a jerk.

**The *Cat* this year lacks a certain happiness and for this,[sic]
we must apologize. It seems that the only grin you'll find in
this book is the one that remains when the Cheshire Cat's
body has fully disappeared.**

Groan.

I submitted a poem of my own to *The Cheshire Cat*. It was prose
poetry. Amazingly, I accepted my poem that I submitted to myself.

The poem was a no-bullshit glance into the depths of human darkness. When I wrote the poem, I read it out loud to my mom. She laughed. I had no idea why and was very hurt. Now I think I see the humor.

THE APARTMENT BUILDING
by Michael Showalter

Curious title considering that the closest I'd ever been to an apartment building was visiting my sister's college dormitory.

> *There is a whore in my apartment building,*
> *Her room smells like dirty sex.*

This is what they call starting big.

> *There is a man next door who reads the comics.*
> *His idea of a hero is a hand job and a beer.*

"Hero" is a double entendre: either a hoagie or an idol.

> *There is a dog in that man's room,*
> *His name is "Asshole" and he smells like piss.*

Word for word, I swear.

> *Across the courtyard, a couple lives.*
> *He's an actor—she's an actress.*
> *They can't find work so they steal from the market.*

The market? Suddenly, we're in Marrakech? What are they stealing from this market? Figs? Spices? Lanyards?

> *I smoked a reefer with them.*

It's not bad enough that I said "reefer." I had to say "a reefer." I don't know that there even is such a thing as "a reefer."

A manuscript lies on a naked mattress
That lies in the corner of my two-room apartment.

Now we're learning more about the narrator. He's a writer! And he lives in a "two-room apartment." No den? No conversation pit? No game room?

It has a coffee stain on it.
The publishers and editors have fucked it all to hell.

Okay. So apparently he's got a book deal.

A six-string guitar rests against a chair in my room. It only has
    three strings.
I'm strung out on dope.

Why not take some of the book deal money and go buy new strings?

Next door to me a young man is writing pamphlets,
They are anti-Semitic.
But for Chrissakes that man is a JEW!

That is very ironic.

A guy lies on a flat surface smoking a cigarette.
I lie dead in my bathtub.

Huh? The End. Thankfully.

Reflections on a Snowy Morning

(a work in progress)

I was inspired to write some poetry for this book. The poem I wrote is called "Reflections on a Snowy Morning." It's a work-in-progress, and I've left my notes in the text so you can see how a great poem is written. (See also "Bonus Poems," p. 65)

REFLECTIONS ON A SNOWY MORNING
a poem by Michael Showalter

It snowed this morning.
Bright and wondrous morning!
Oh wondrous snowy day!
The flakes were so light and fluffy
Like really good fucking pancakes.

Note to self: By "really good fucking pancakes," I do not mean two pancakes fucking. Pancakes don't fuck. At least not that I'm aware of. (Search online to see if there are any sexually active pancakes.)

Note to self: Consider cutting the word *fucking* and just have it read "The flakes were so light and fluffy like really good pancakes."

Little speckles of fluffy flakes

Cascading like rose petals
Onto the street below my apartment.

Note to self: *Flakes* rhymes with *cakes*. Do I want this? Think of synonyms for *flakes*: *chunks* or *blobs*.

Hitting the pavement
Like plops of really tiny cat doody
Hitting a litter box.

Note to self: Instead of "hitting," maybe put in "*would* hit a litter box." In other words, "Hitting the pavement like plops of really tiny cat doody *would* hit a litter box" as opposed to just "hitting." In any event, the point is that the snow is hitting the pavement in a similar way that tiny cat doody would.

Million-dollar question to self: All of this is assuming that cat doody falls from the sky; to my knowledge, it doesn't. To say nothing of the fact that "tiny cat doody" as such isn't necessarily something that actually exists.

Note to self: Find out if tiny cat doody is something that actually exists. Check New York Library or Strand Bookstore. Or just google. Gut tells me no on cat doody question. Are there other types of small doody if cat falls through? Frog doody? Bird doody? Poetic license is possibility here. Get feedback from friends. You're too inside the poem to know what's best. Leave tiny cat doody in for now. Maybe if you cut tiny cat doody, you'll make new discoveries. Revisit this. Additionally, and this is something to really think about: Is *doody* poetic enough of a word? Other words in consideration are *crud* and *fecal matter*. *Fecal matter* seems too clinical. *Crud* is solid but doesn't roll off the tongue like *doody*. Ew! That sounds gross. "Rolls off the tongue like doody." Ha. Anyway, of the three, *doody* has most resonance. Put pin in *doody* debate.

Reminder to self: Writing is rewriting!!!!!

> *The pitter-patter of snowy doo-doo*
> *Tiny cat poop flakes*
> *Falling on the street*
> *Like plops of poop on my feet.*

Note to self: "Feet" is bookmark. Other word will go there that rhymes with *street*. "Feet" will do for now. Also, I'm wondering about "snowy doo-doo makes pitter-patter sound."

Note to self: Find out if snowy doo-doo makes pitter-patter sound. Check *Plattler Almanac* and/or *Husker's Glossary of Weather Sounds*— check Manitoba Institute website for avail. Or just google.

Bonus Poems

BUMS (AS IN TUSHIES) AND TWINE
By Michael Showalter

Bums and twine
Bums and twine
One is bums.
The other is twine.
Bums and twine.
Bums and twine.
One is bums
The other is twine.
Bums and twine
Bums
And twine.

BUMMIES AND TWISTLE
By Michael Showalter

Bummies and twistle
Bummies and twistle
Bales of bummies
And whistling twistle
Bummies and twistle
Bummies and twistle
There goes the bummies

And the whistling twistle!
What ho! Bummies!
What ho! Twistle!
Bummies and twistle
And bales of bummies.
Bummies and twistle
And whistling pine.
Bummies and twistle
And bummies.

SPOTS AND BIFFLES
By Michael Showalter

Spots and biffles
Biffles and spots
Spots and biffles
Biffles and spots
One is biffles
The other is spots
Spots and biffles
And whiffling spots
Sniffling spots
Rhymes with biffles
Sniffles does.
And spots.
And whiffling biffles
And spots.

FERNS AND BIFFLES (UNFINISHED)
By Michael Showalter

Fernies and biffles and whistling biffles
Biffles and ferns and whistling biffles

Fiffles and biffles and whistling biffles
Ferns and biffles and whistling spots.
And biffles and…
(And then I stopped writing this poem.)

How to Write and Sell a Hollywood Screenplay

Chapter One

Quick and Easy Instructions

1. Write the script really, really fast
2. Get on over to Hollywood and sell it
3. Be nudged out of rewriting process by studio
4. Complain to loved ones about "integrity" of your idea being compromised
5. Sue Writers Guild of America to retain sole writing credit
6. Attend premiere and have out-of-body experience watching your script come to life on "the big screen"
7. Take a series of meetings to sell your next idea
8. Get offer to buy that idea with caveat that you'll change everything about it
9. Consult with loved ones on how to proceed
10. Take the money/buy bigger home
11. Struggle with writer's block
12. Begin psychoanalysis to unblock your creativity
13. Notice that soul slips out of your body intermittently and at unexpected moments
14. Join self-help cult to get soul back
15. Rise through cult and stop hanging out with old friends
16. Sell three more scripts in a two-week period

17. Hire personal trainer and become amateur kickboxer
18. Buy ranch in Montana
19. Turn into a ball of light and float into space
20. Realize that you are not a ball of light or in space but have gone crazy and are in a mental inpatient facility
21. Discover that self-help cult leader has stolen all your money
22. Be on network reality show/dancing competition to pay off lawyer's fees

Alternate Instructions for People Who Are in Less of a Rush

1. Think of original idea
2. Create memorable characters
3. Take time writing script
4. Consider it labor of love

My Morning Routine, #2

There was a recent news story here in New York City that people were complaining about a mysterious "maple syrup smell" that wafted over them. The mayor held a news conference to announce that "with the help of hundreds of law enforcement agents" they'd discovered that the maple syrup smell was coming from a nearby factory that made... maple syrup! After hearing this I thought, "Ah, so that's where the smell is coming from. The maple syrup factory nearby." And New Yorkers rejoiced: "We no longer have to contend with the yummy brunch smell! We get to smell the rancid garbage again!"

Another New York news story that caught my attention involved the rapper 50 Cent and a free concert that he was giving in his old Brooklyn neighborhood. The city was worried about gang violence and the mayor put out a press release saying, "People are encouraged to have fun, sing and dance, but you're not allowed to shoot anyone."

Some words aren't right. Like in baseball, when you throw the ball at another player's face, it's called *beaning*. People have been seriously injured as a result of beaning. It can be lethal. To me *beaning* should be the word for throwing an actual bean at someone's face, like maybe a lima bean or a snow pea, not a really hard baseball going a hundred miles per hour.

Speaking of baseball, I thought of a funny way to change the words to a famous song of our national pastime. "Take me out to the ballgame, take me out to the park! Buy me some penis and Cracker Jacks! I don't care if I ever get back!" Hahhahhahaahh! I said *penis*!

Would Thanksgiving be as popular of a holiday if it were called *Turkeybutt Party*?

I like making up different words for things. Like when I go to the movies I always like to subtly mispronounce the name of the movie I'm buying tickets for. It's very subtle. Not mean-spirited at all. Like I went to see the Matt Damon movie *The Good Shepherd* and I ordered tickets to see *The Good Shepherd's Pie*. Which I thought was HILARIOUS. The ticket person didn't even seem to notice. I keep doing it at the candy counter too. I ordered a bag of Twizzles. The woman behind the counter gave me this look like, "Fucking asshole thinks that Twizzlers are called Twizzles."

The Universal Theme
of Adolescence

This morning I thought I was truly ready to write. First, I showered, then I made the bed ("messy bed, messy head"), and I got coffee. I did all of the things I promised myself I would do. I was ready. No more excuses.

I sat down at my desk. I opened my laptop. I turned it on. I plugged my stereo into the computer and put on some "work music"—*Unforgettable Fire* by U2 on constant repeat. I opened a blank document and I titled it "Book." I pressed the return button a bunch of times and did a "quote page" because all books have quote pages. Then I pressed Save As and I saved the file as "Quote Page."

The first quote I did was a Bob Dylan lyric. Everyone does Bob Dylan quotes so I did too. "Hey! Mr. Tambourine Man, play a song for me." This was a good quote, totally meaningless to me, but good, so I added another one just for good measure. This time it was not a Bob Dylan quote. "Don't shoot 'til you see the whites of their eyes!" Someone said that during the Revolutionary War.[10] And a third quote, "It ain't the size of the boat that counts. It's the motion of the ocean." My old high school friend Richard used to say that.

---

10. William Prescott said it to his troops because he didn't want them to waste ammunition, the idea being to only take shots that would kill the British soldiers. General Israel Putnam said it before Prescott at the Battle of Breed's Hill and Prescott repeated it. The quote was originally said by Frederick II, King of Prussia. So basically every guy with a set of vocal cords is reported to have said this at one point or another. (For more on the American Revolution, see "Two Generals' Problem" at the end of this chapter.)

I saved the quote page file, then I went back to my file called "Book." I was back looking at a totally blank page. I decided to write out my "Thank You" page. I wrote: "For Amelia, my lovely wife of forty years. Tobias and Evelyn, my beautiful children. Scooter, my chocolate Labrador, and all seventeen of our chickens at our farm that we have. This book is for you."

I pressed Save As and titled the file "Thank You Page." I knew that there was no "Amelia," no "Tobias and Evelyn," no "Scooter," no "farm," and no "chickens." I figured I could go back and change it when I knew whom I wanted to thank. I checked my page count and saw that I had already, and in such short order, written two pages of my book. The thought even crossed my mind, "This is easy."

Returning to my file "Book," I knew it was now time to start writing the actual book part. "Here I go," I thought. "Here I go about to write a twelve-hundred-page novel." I typed the words "My Adolescence." Then I added a : (colon, not the ass-part, the punctuation mark). I hit return and then I tabbed. Then I closed my eyes, wiggled my fingers, and waited for the words to come. Nothing. I wiggled them some more. Sometimes my fingers take a few extra wiggles to get fired up. Nothing. Then I watched the icon blinking, taunting me, mocking me. It was waiting for me to write something else. I couldn't write. I had writer's block. I felt a wave of nausea come over me, like I might puke, so I went into the bedroom and played *Madden Football* on my Xbox for three hours.

When I returned three hours later, thumb and forefinger heavily bruised from attacking the joystick as though it were a punching bag, I wrote:

The universal theme of adolescence is acceptance. Some people crave it while others rebel against it. I craved it. I wanted to be popular, and the key to being popular was fitting in. I didn't have that key.

I liked that. It sounded very "novelistic." At that point I went for a long walk.

When I returned from my walk, I sat on my sofa and watched television.

I felt bad about this and wondered, "Why aren't I writing?" Then I heard a voice. The voice said, "You have to be at your computer to write."

I went over to my computer, turned it back on, and checked my email.

Then I surfed the net.

Then I checked my email more.

Then I resurfed the net.

Then I heard the voice again, "Once at your computer, open your file called 'Book.' And write!" So I did.

In my eighth-grade middle school yearbook there's a "Who's Who" section in the back, where we vote for each other in a list of categories. For each category, there is a boy and a girl winner. It's like my middle school's version of the Academy Awards.

1. *Best Looking*
2. *Most Popular*
3. *Best Personality*
4. *Class Flirt*
5. *Most Outgoing*
6. *Nicest Smile*
7. *Class Clown*
8. *Most Humorous*
9. *Most Athletic*
10. *Best Dressed*

I really want to win Most Humorous. Class Clown would be acceptable, but Class Clown is as much of an award for being "class asshole" as it is an award for being funny. Most former Class Clown award winners from my middle school are juvenile delinquents and arsonists.

And it's true. Kids were constantly burning things down in Princeton. It seemed like every week some kid got shipped off to boarding school because he or she "burned down his parents' house."

It's coming to the end of eighth grade, and I've been thinking about the Who's Who Awards since the third grade, when I first saw them in my older sister's yearbook.

My sister didn't win anything, but that was because she was smart and they didn't have an award for that. Awards for being smart came later in life, in the form of college acceptance letters and lucrative job offers after obtaining multiple degrees.

In my middle school, the popular crowd completely rules the school, and gaining acceptance into their fold isn't easy. Lineage is a factor; wardrobe is a factor; size of house is a factor; being good at "lax" (lacrosse) is a factor; even where you went to elementary school is a factor.

After fifth grade, Princeton's four elementary schools were combined into one school. Each elementary school had its own distinct persona:

Littlebrook: That's where I went. The school was like the name— unassuming, and little.

Riverside: Riverside was where all the children of hippies went. Riverside kids were feral and arty. All of their clothes had that spice rack + "Dad smokes pot in the house" smell.

Community Park: All of the troubled kids wound up there. Every month or so some kid tried to burn the school down.

Johnson Park: Johnson Park was on the outskirts of town. It was where the rich, beautiful kids went. They were the popular kids from day one.

The Johnson Park kids started having boy/girl parties early on in sixth grade. Being invited to one of these parties was a sign of having "made it" socially. I got invited to some of them and *for five seconds in sixth grade I was popular.*

I'm standing in front of my bathroom mirror. It's Friday night and I'm going to a boy/girl party. I'm drenching my body in Polo cologne, and I have this feeling of excitement. It's a dangerous, anything-can-happen sort of feeling. I am growing up. I am a fuck-machine.

Not true. Lost virginity a thousand years later. It happened in college. I was drunk. She was drunk. I had expected losing my virginity to be something like a scene from *9½ Weeks*. It was more sort of a just-mash-it-in-there kind of moment.

We're all assembled in Pam Litvak's basement, eating candy and cheese balls. Someone puts on that song "Our House" by Madness, and we all start dancing around crazy, like pogo sticks. My friend Roger is telling me to ask Heather Crandall to "go out." She's really preppy. I like her. She's standing on the stairwell. I'm pogo sticking. Roger knees me in the back and I stop dancing and I walk over to her and I ask her out by whispering in her ear, "Hey, Heather. Will you go out with me?"

That's how it worked back then. You asked someone to "go out with you." I had no idea what it meant. I still don't. It presumes you have to "go out" somewhere. What if you want to stay in? I suppose you could ask, "Do you want to stay in with me?" But then you've got the inverse problem, because if you ask someone to "stay in" with you, does that mean you can't go out? This is why relationships are so difficult.

Back then, first base meant making out. Second base meant feeling up. Third base meant fingering. Home run meant intercourse. Until college, I only ever went to first base because I wanted to hit for average. At parties and after school, kids were always retreating to the woods to have sex. For those of you who grew up in a city, think of the woods as the back stairwell in an apartment building. The woods were a big problem for me because I wasn't "outdoorsy." Whenever I think of the woods I think of rotting tree trunks, and the idea of hooking up with a girl on a pile of wet leaves didn't turn me on. I wanted to hook up in less exotic locations, like on the sofa or in a warm bed or in an upside-down swing.

We used to play a game at parties called I Never. The way it worked was that you'd say something starting with "I never" and then you'd say something sexual. If you had done the thing that was said, then you'd drink. The other kids were so much more advanced than me. They'd say things like "I've never had sex in one of the classrooms after school." And then everyone would drink! I hadn't even had a sandwich in one of the classrooms after school. But I didn't want people to think that I was a virgin, so I would drink too. But they all knew that I was lying, and someone would ask whom I'd done it with and I'd say, "Chick from a different school, you wouldn't know her. She's a ballet dancer, spends most of her time in the city." And when it was my turn, to avoid more humiliation, I'd say something nonsexual like, "I've never read two Stephen King novels in a row." Then I'd pound.

Before I started masturbating, I had wet dreams. While other boys were running into the bathroom between classes to masturbate, I was running into the bathroom to take naps. In the beginning, I would take three or four naps a day. One day my mom caught me napping. I was so embarrassed.

So Heather and I are standing there. I'm thinking: What does this mean now that we're "going out"? Where will we go?! I don't know any good places. I mean, there's always Vesuvio's (a pizza place) and of course Hoagie Haven. It is a dangerous, anything-can-happen sort of feeling.

We smile at each other, neither one of us knowing what to say. It's awkward. Now that we are "very much together," it seems like all of the mystery and tension between us has evaporated.

We do not speak again that night or ever again for the rest of our lives. She eventually burned her parents' house down and was sent to boarding school.

A few months later, a bunch of the seventh grader boys come to one
of the parties and bring a case of beer. I refuse to drink. I am too
scared. All of the popular girls scorn me. After that I am banished
from the middle school popular crowd. I turn back into a pumpkin.
My five seconds has expired.

I've realized that I don't like parties. Like, a few weeks ago, I was at
a downtown New York party surrounded by "artists and intellectuals."
At first I thought to myself, "I *want* this. I *want* this way of life. I *want*
to be the guy in the crushed velvet blazer and the silk blouse talking
about 'metaphysics' and 'Proust' and 'the dialectic.'" But the truth is
that I don't know what any of that means. Who's Proust? Does he have
a Huffington Post blog? If so, I've probably read him, but if he doesn't,
then I'm not much of an addition to the conversation.

Everyone at the party looks good in that "I'm just dirty enough to
look like I don't care but this belt buckle once belonged to the Prince
of Spain" kind of way. I'm holding a glass of "port" and I'm pretending that I don't wish it were a glass of Hawaiian Punch and I'm trying
really hard to seem smart, and into burlesque, and curious about what
Brian Wilson's music really *means* and I'm thinking to myself, "What's
port?"

I'm standing near the imported cheese plate, wishing it was imported
from Wisconsin and not Italy because it tastes kind of like a fart, and
I'm overhearing the woman next to me talking about how she went to
India to find herself and now she's humble and getting more "shows"
than ever and I'm thinking, "How can you be humble if you're bragging about all your shows?" And then I'm thinking, "What 'shows' is
she talking about? And why did you need to go to India to find yourself?
Last time I checked, people were dying in the streets in India. Is that
where you found yourself, in a pile of dead bodies?"

Next thing I know we're all being shuffled into the living room for an
impromptu performance. It's a hipster husband and wife. He plays tuba
and she plays the accordion. They start playing and everyone has their

eyes closed and people are all nodding their heads like something really deep and important is happening. To me they sound like a moose fucking a goose. Their "impromptu performance" lasts over an hour and forty minutes—not including encores.

Oh shit, here come the guys with the beards. Everywhere I look I see guys with beards. They look like that *brewmeister* in the Sam Adams commercials! You know the guy I'm talking about? He's wearing fishing waders and he's got short hair and a ZZ Top beard.

Apparently this is the new look for guys these days. It's the "Civil War Soldier" look. Don't these guys realize that men died in that war? Aren't their faces scratchy? And it seems like all of them either make junk sculptures or are starting their own smokehouse or something. Don't they have jobs? Why are they talking to me about how they're learning how to "smoke fish"? I'm like, "Dude, how about instead of smoking fish you use your liberal arts education to shave your fucking beard off!" And then they walk away and join the group of girls with bangs, and now I'm left alone over by the fart cheese, thinking about the Civil War and smoked fish.

At some point, I'd had enough and I snuck downstairs and went out onto the street to catch my breath. I hailed the first cab I saw, and as I was riding over the Brooklyn Bridge, I could see downtown disappearing behind me.

But baack (not a typo) to eighth grade: In addition to the "Who's Who" section in the yearbook, we were given a "Likes and Dislikes" questionnaire to fill out, the answers for which would accompany our photograph. I recall filling out this form and not wanting to rock the boat. I wanted to "like" what everyone else liked. I wanted to "dislike" what everyone else disliked.

My "Likes" Were

1. Pizza
2. Cute Girls

3. Ska Music
4. Parties
5. LAX (Lacrosse)

My Dislikes Were

1. Homework
2. Mondays
3. Lame Parties
4. Cornballs
5. The Bee Gees

I figured that if I followed suit, then people would *like* me more and *dislike* me less. I wanted to be accepted. It didn't work. Even my own friends disowned me.

I'm at the bike racks outside of school. My friends are all marching off somewhere and I yell after them, "Hey guys! Wait up!" They turn around, arms folded.

"You're not invited," says Nick, the pack leader.

"Why not?" I ask. I look at my other friends for backup, but they stand silently behind Nick, staring at their shoes.

"We've decided that we don't like you anymore," Nick says. All my friends close rank behind him, nodding. He digs in. "You're a spaz," he says. "And you're corny."

He smirks. They all laugh.

Spaz *and* corny *are the worst things you could ever say to someone. I want to die.*

My friends put me on "double secret probation" and treated me like a second-class citizen for a few months before granting me "full-friend" status again. I had to "behave" in order to be reinstated. The groveling made me feel like my soul had been sucked out of my butthole. Winning Most Humorous in the yearbook would be my revenge!

We receive our "Who's Who" ballots on little slips of paper in homeroom one morning. I already know which person I'm going to choose for each category, but I don't want to fill it out too fast. I don't want to give the impression that it is vitally important to me, or a matter of life and death, or something that occupies my every waking thought, so I put the ballot in my pocket and wait.

The next day I talk to my friend Ellen, who is on the student council. She says that they need help counting the votes for "Who's Who." I volunteer to help her under the false pretense of being a generous and giving person. We count the votes in a small stockroom filled with school supplies and folding chairs in the basement of the school.

Ballot after ballot, my name does not come up.

Out of over 250 ballots, I do not receive a single vote for Most Humorous. I get two votes for Nicest Smile. Fuck nicest smile.

I justify my poor showing by telling myself that it is just a "popularity contest," which it is, but that doesn't make it an easier pill to swallow. It just means that, save for the two people who like my smile, I'm not popular.

IN RETROSPECT

My True "Likes" Were

1. Broadway Musicals
2. Weird Girls
3. John Belushi
4. *Mork & Mindy*
5. Break Dancing

My True "Dislikes" Were

1. Homework of Any Kind
2. Being Told by My Friends That They Didn't Like Me Anymore

3. My Burgeoning Pubes
4. My Nose, Which Grew Far Faster Than Any Other Part of My Body
5. The Popular Crowd

A STATISTICAL ANALYSIS OF MY MIDDLE SCHOOL YEARBOOK "LIKES AND DISLIKES"

Boys' "Likes"

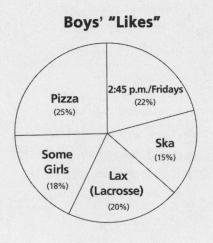

Pizza (25%)
2:45 p.m./Fridays (22%)
Ska (15%)
Some Girls (18%)
Lax (Lacrosse) (20%)

Boys' "Dislikes"

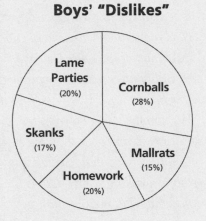

Lame Parties (20%)
Cornballs (28%)
Skanks (17%)
Mallrats (15%)
Homework (20%)

Girls' "Likes"

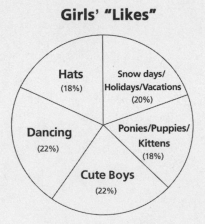

Hats (18%)
Snow days/ Holidays/Vacations (20%)
Dancing (22%)
Ponies/Puppies/ Kittens (18%)
Cute Boys (22%)

Girls' "Dislikes"

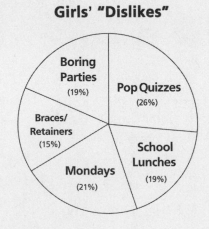

Boring Parties (19%)
Pop Quizzes (26%)
Braces/ Retainers (15%)
School Lunches (19%)
Mondays (21%)

A STATISTICAL ANALYSIS OF MY MIDDLE SCHOOL
YEARBOOK "LIKES AND DISLIKES"

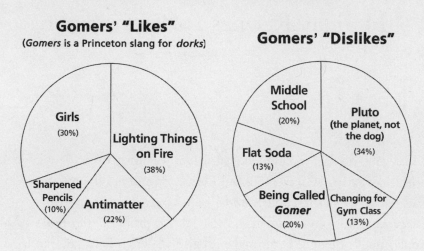

Gomers' "Likes"
(*Gomers* is a Princeton slang for *dorks*)

Girls (30%)

Lighting Things on Fire (38%)

Sharpened Pencils (10%)

Antimatter (22%)

Gomers' "Dislikes"

Middle School (20%)

Pluto (the planet, not the dog) (34%)

Flat Soda (13%)

Being Called *Gomer* (20%)

Changing for Gym Class (13%)

Holiday Recipes for Gentlemen

I like cooking. Let me amend that: I like watching other people cook and I like eating cooked food. But I really do respect the culinary arts. I watch *Top Chef* religiously and I never pass up an opportunity at a fancy restaurant to comment on the "flavor profiles." I'm not a great cook myself, though. I can make spaghetti, which is to say that I can boil water. I can make toast. I can peel an orange. That's about it. Still, I strive but I just don't have the "touch." You gotta have that "touch." I cooked dinner for my family over Thanksgiving and surprisingly it went over really well. I saved my recipes and thought I'd put them in writing for my fellow "non-cooks."

Punkin Pie

This is actually just pumpkin pie but pronounced in a funny way. The *mp* is replaced with an *n* to give it a down-home feel. It doesn't matter if it tastes good. You'll get laughs and admiration for calling it "punkin pie." Check any recipe book for cooking directions.

Mashed Potatoes

- Buy a bunch of potatoes.
- Take them out of the bag and put them in a pot filled with water.
- Boil them.
- Go about your business for a pretty long time.
- Periodically poke them with a fork to see if they're soft.

- When they feel soft, drain the water out of the pot.
- With the same fork you poked them with earlier, mash up the potatoes in the pot.

Green Beans

- Go to any supermarket frozen food section.
- Buy a bag of frozen green beans.
- Go home and take out a frying pan. If you don't have a frying pan, you can use a pot.
- Put the frozen green beans in the pan.
- Turn on the heat and poke the beans with a fork until they don't seem frozen anymore.
- Repeat this until you think they're done.

Loaf of French Bread

- Go to a deli and buy a loaf of French bread.
- When you get home, take the bread out of the bag and cut it into slices with a knife. If you don't have any clean knives, you can simply rip the bread apart with your hands.
- Put pieces of bread in a bowl and serve.

Gravy

- Go to your local supermarket and ask the guy where the canned gravy is.
- Go get the canned gravy. Buy it.
- Open the canned gravy with a can opener. If you don't have a can opener, you can use a bottle opener by puncturing lots of holes in the top and then prying the top off with a hammer.
- Put the gravy in a saucepan. If you have no saucepan, you can use a frying pan or any kind of pot.
- Heat it. Periodically dip your fingers in gravy and taste it.

- When you think it's done, put it in a gravy boat and serve it. If you don't have a gravy boat, you can put it in a bowl.
- Put a nice serving spoon in the gravy boat. If you don't have a serving spoon, you can use any kind of spoon—or even a fork if you don't have any clean spoons.

Pecan Pie

- Go to dessert shop and purchase a box of pecan pie.
- Ask for their best one.
- Take it home. Cut out a slice and eat it to make sure it's good.
- Cut out another slice and eat it to double-check.
- Eat one piece before bed tonight.
- Eat another piece after that.
- Eat a piece for breakfast tomorrow morning.
- Take remaining pieces, wrap in plastic, hide in fridge for later.
- Think of way to explain to guests that you didn't have time to make a dessert.
- Ask friends to bring ice cream.

Turduckenburgerdog

Ingredients:
- 1 turkey (12 lbs.)
- 1 duck (5 lbs.)
- 1 chicken (4 lbs.)
- 1 hamburger bun
- 1 hot dog

Cooking Directions:
- Stuff the hot dog in the chicken's butt. Stuff the chicken up the duck's butt. Stuff the duck with the chicken up its butt up the turkey's butt.
- Let simmer.
- When it's done, put the whole thing on a hamburger bun.

Employees Must Wash Hands

Every restaurant has this sign in their restroom.

> **Employees must wash hands before returning to work.**

That got me wondering. What would that same sign say in a Chinese restaurant?

> **Employees must wash hands before returning to wok.**

And then I started thinking, what would that sign look like in a Scandinavian restaurant?

> **Employees must flarn pans before exploring the pork.**

And then I thought—what would that sign look like in a Belgian restaurant?

> **Empoilees moost warpsh anz burfur termning firps.**

And that got me thinking. What would the sign say in a different kind of restaurant?

Rubby's fuss and bacon eager warbling to work.

And then I thought...

Toomies purmner flang in wub noodles turds . . . or SHIMS!

Which got me thinking...

Sandle *bag* wooden poop jangling flubber doodle.

And then I thought...

Poop jangling is kind of like other kinds of jangling but instead of jangling with other kinds of things you jangle with poop.

And then I thought...

I like poop jangling b/c it's good for movement and voice, which helps me with auditions for small parts in movies such as *Signs* by M. Night Shyamalan.

And then I thought...

I'm taking a poop jangling seminar at Juilliard from famous poop jangler Pierre LaFarge, who recently poop jangled with Cirque du Soleil in their new show *Shampoo . . . au . . . eu.*

And then I'm thinking...

HELP!!!!!!!!!! I'M TRAPPED INSIDE THIS BIT!!!!!!!!

And then I'm thinking...

MUST GET OUT!

And now I'm thinking...

THINK, MICHAEL, THINK

And...

Come on, Michael...

And...

YOU CAN DO IT!

And...

I BELIEEEEEEVE IN YOU!!!!!

Then I have a thought!

WAIT!

I have it!

DUCK with a penis!

And now I'm relieved.

THE END.

This bit was...

Directed by Joel and Ethan Coen

How to Write and Sell a Hollywood Screenplay

Chapter Two

THE RULE OF THREES

One of the most essential rules of comedy is the Rule of Threes. This rule states that jokes work best in threes. There is no scientific explanation for this, other than that it is time tested and seems to be true. For example, here's a fictional "to do" list. For the purposes of experimentation, let's start with a two-item list:

To Do

1. Laundry
2. Go to hardware store

Not very funny, right? And that's because comedy doesn't work in twos. Why? *Doesn't matter.* It just doesn't. Now, let's add a third item to the list, and see if we don't get a different result:

To Do

1. Laundry
2. Go to hardware store
3. Boogers??!!

You died just now from laughing so hard, right? The Rule of Threes always delivers.

A Note to My Skeptic Friend: Maybe you're thinking, "It's only funnier because *boogers* is a cheap laugh funny word. To say nothing of the fact that all of the question marks and exclamation points are sort of telegraphing the joke." Okay fair enough, but let's look at the list with only two items again and see if we still feel this way:

To Do

1. Laundry
2. Boogers??!!

That wasn't as funny as when it went *laundry, hardware store,* and then *boogers??!!* Was it? And this is not a matter of opinion. I am stating facts.

Some of us are unwilling to give in to the Rule of Threes, and for us there is a lesser-known rule, the Rule of Sevens. This rule also works well. It was popular during the Dutch Renaissance, but over time, as our attention spans grew shorter, our patience for the Rule of Sevens grew shorter as well. The Rule of Threes became the accepted rule, and the Rule of Sevens, which reigned supreme during the Dutch Renaissance and parts of the Prussian Schism, became obsolete.

Let's go back to our fake "to do" list to see how the Rule of Sevens applies:

To Do

1. Laundry
2. Go to hardware store
3. Return emails
4. Make phone calls
5. Boogers??!!

6. Go to the gym
7. Pick up framed poster

In the Rule of Sevens the punch line comes at number five.
Here are a few more examples:

Top Seven Best Rock Bands of All Time

1. The Beatles
2. The Rolling Stones
3. The Police
4. Radiohead
5. Hoobastank??!!
6. The Pretenders
7. The Beach Boys

Top Seven Best Movies of All Time

1. *Citizen Kane*
2. *Casablanca*
3. *Rear Window*
4. *Breathless*
5. *Porky's??!!*
6. *Seven Samurai*
7. *Persona*

Top Seven Best TV Shows of All Time

1. *Cheers*
2. *The Office*
3. *M*A*S*H*
4. *All in the Family*

5. *Jersey Shore??!!*
6. *The Cosby Show*
7. *Hill Street Blues*

Some comedians still use the Rule of Sevens. These comedians are considered purists. I myself have dabbled in both the Rule of Threes and the Rule of Sevens.

Below is a piece I wrote incorporating the Rule of Threes. It's a piece entitled "My Apartment and What It Looks Like and Frogs??!!!!"

"MY APARTMENT AND WHAT IT LOOKS LIKE AND FROGS??!!!!"
(A short piece that incorporates the Rule of Threes)
by Michael Showalter

My apartment is fairly small, a bit cluttered, and hot buttered waffle??!! On my desk, I have a computer, a printer, and bags of poop??!!

Now, way lesser known than even the Rule of Sevens is the Rule of Twelves. The Rule of Twelves, or *Twelving* as it was called during its era (the rule of Charlemagne), involved a joke coming on the fourth, ninth, and twelfth lines of a piece of comedy. Here's an example of Twelving from an ancient text. The scribe, Lord Brownby, was a well-known humorist of his era and the foremost Twelver of his time. His most popular Twelve was performed, or so say the history books, one thousand and fifty times before the king. (Not Charlemagne, though. A different king, King Boriz of Issterland.) Here is Brownby's famous poem. The lines are numbered so you can see how a Twelve works.

My Larder Board: A Twelver, by Lord Brownby

1. *My larder board is filled with larder*
2. *In it I have pickled and candied food, I do*
3. *Many a duke and duchess have eaten from it, they have*

4. *Except when goosing each other in the bum*
5. *My larder board is well stocked, it is*
6. *Stocked the wellest in the land, it is*
7. *Fresh vegetables and savory meats, it has*
8. *My larder board is the finest in the land, it is*
9. *Except when all the noble folk are in goose mode*
10. *Otherwise, my larder board is well admired*
11. *And well cooked from, I might add*
12. *But when all are goosing each other, the larder board is less well attended to.*

Boxers Box

The hardest part about writing a book for me is that I don't know how *I* write a book. What's my process? Do I write in the morning or do I write at night? Do I write nonstop for hours? Or do I take breaks? What do I wear when I write? Am I fully clothed? Or do I write in the buff?[11] The answer to all these questions is that I *don't know* because I've never written a book before. There are some things about my process that I definitely do know. I know **for a fact** that I like to walk and write at the same time. This is difficult, though, because I have to balance my laptop on one hand while typing with the other. Also, my computer battery runs out quickly so I can only work at short intervals before needing to go home to recharge my laptop battery. Or worse, sometimes I'll abruptly stop walking and then the person behind me bumps into me. This usually leads to a harsh exchange along the lines of, "Hey, asshole, what the fuck!?"

Another part of my process that I know about is that I like taking lots of "writing breaks." I like to work for ten or fifteen minutes and then take a break for an hour or so. The problem with "writing breaks" is that you can't write while you're on a break from writing. I'm wondering if it's possible to write during my "writing breaks," but I feel like that would defeat the purpose of the break. Or would it?! (*Note to self*: Meditate on this question: Could a writer write on a break from writing?)

I came upon another writing quote that I like: "Writers write. Boxers

11. *Buff* refers to a soft, thick, undyed leather made from the skin of a buffalo. That's not how I meant it, though. I meant *naked*. Or more colloquially, *nekkid*.

box." This makes sense to me. If you're a boxer, you box. If you're a writer, you write. It's not rocket science. In other words, boxers don't question themselves because they don't have time. They fight. It's simple. Why should there be any difference with writing? Then again, I guess, it's easier to know if you're a good boxer because if you look across the ring and the face of the guy you're fighting against looks like a bowl of ground beef, then you know you're doing well. However, if what you're writing looks like a bowl of ground beef, then I think you're in trouble, so it's sort of paradoxical. (*Question to self*: Does what I'm writing look like a bowl of ground beef?)

It's 1986, I'm a sophomore in high school, and I'm visiting my sister at Yale. On the first night, she takes me to see the Whiffenpoofs, the popular all-male a cappella singing group on campus.

It used to be that a cappella singing groups mostly sang old songs like "Oh Danny Boy" and "Shenandoah," but in the Eighties they were starting to do a cappella arrangements of more modern songs.

The night I see them, the Whiffenpoofs do a very memorable doo-wop rendition of "Jesse's Girl" by Rick Springfield.

I love singing. Back when I was in middle school I sang tenor in the choir, and one winter, I was given a solo line in "We Wish You a Merry Christmas." My solo came two stanzas in: "Oh, bring us some figgy pudding! Oh, bring us some figgy pudding! Oh, bring us some figgy pudding and a cup of good cheer!" I belted out my line like a soloist in an opera. The whole time, I'm thinking, "What the fuck is figgy pudding?"

Figgy pudding is a spice cake made with figs and walnuts.

As I listen to the Whiffenpoofs sing a somber rendition of "Barracuda" by Heart, I try to imagine myself singing a cappella when I go to college. I like the idea of being in some sort of group,

but doo-wopping feels a bit corny to me. I just can't see myself
bouncing around with a bunch of dudes, snapping my fingers,
my legs all jangly, singing Eighties hits in four-part harmony.

The night before I left, my sister took me to see the improv troupe on campus, the Purple Crayon. Their show was in a dingy basement in one of the Yale residence halls. There were twenty or so folding chairs set up around a makeshift stage with crappy lighting. Everyone drank red wine out of Dixie cups.

They are like rock stars to me! They are having so much fun and
acting utterly silly. Silly!!! I am used to my life in Princeton, where
people judge you by the way you tie your shoes, and here are a
bunch of smart guys acting really stupid, loping around on a stage
without a care in the world. I decide then and there that I want to
be in a comedy group one day.

A few months later, back in high school, I tried improv for myself when I was in the ensemble cast of the musical *The Threepenny Opera*. I played one of the "townspeople." No small parts, only small actors.

Our director was the theater teacher at school. He had a salt-and-pepper beard and smoked a pipe. He smelled like rutabaga, black coffee, and curry. He wore turtlenecks. He spoke with a transatlantic accent and told us tales of being in "off-Broadway plays" as a younger man. Rumors swirled that he had a kilo of Turkish hash in his freezer at home. We were all very impressed by him.

We're at rehearsal one afternoon and he says, "Today we're going
to do an improvisation." I had seen that improv group at my sister's
college and loved them, but I had never done an "improvisation"
myself and I am filled with nervous excitement.
He gathers us together on the stage and says that we should
pretend that we are in Victorian London. He asks us to imagine
the streets and the smells, the old buildings, the merchants selling

goods to each other. He tells us to begin by walking around on the stage and letting our minds wander.

I've been to London. London smells like the plague. It smells like the Blitz, Jack the Ripper, and the plague.

After a few minutes of walking and imagining, the director calls out to us, "Imagine that something's about to go down!" We all pause. What does he mean?

"What do you mean?" someone finally asks.

"Something's going to go down! On the streets!*"*

Oh, "on the streets," I think. I still don't know what he means. No one does.

"Go! Go! Go!" he calls out to us.

We continue walking around in a circle. I walk up to someone and say, "Hey, um, so something's about to go down."

And then the other person says, "Really?"

And then I say, "Yep. Something's going to go down."

And then they say, "What is it?"

And then I say, "Not sure but it's happening on the streets." Then we nod at each other and keep walking.

Our director sits in the audience watching us, gleaming with pride.

The Joys of Streaking

I can't tell you how many times I've put on my shoes, put on a scarf, taken off my underwear, put on a beret, put on a pair of mittens, taken off my shirt, and run a nude lap around the block for all to see. Yep, there's nothing I love so much on a cold night as a good old-fashioned streak.

What exactly is *streaking* you ask? Well, through my extensive research at ~~the New York Public Library, the Library of Congress, Princeton University's Firestone Library, the Smithsonian Institution, the Huntington Library in California, and~~ Wikipedia I learned that the first recorded incident of streaking by a college student in the United States occurred in 1804 at Washington College (now Washington and Lee University) when a senior named George William Crump was arrested for running naked through campus. Crump was suspended for the academic session, but would later go on to become a U.S. congressman and ambassador to Chile.

Streaking can be a very spiritual and freeing experience, but there are certain ground rules. Let's examine the Fundamental Principles of Streaking:

People look funny when they run.
People look funny when they're naked.
Therefore, people look really funny when they run naked.

Conversely:

People who run well don't look funny when they run.

People who look good naked don't look funny when they're naked.
Therefore, people who run well and look good naked may be ill-suited for
*   streaking.*

But:

People who run well but don't look good naked make fine streakers.
People who look good naked but don't run well are also fine streakers.
Therefore, the only requirement for successful streaking is either being
*   a bad runner or looking ugly when naked.*

All that said, here's the good news: Streaking *is* for everyone. Even good-looking people who run well can pull off a successful streak if they've got the right attitude. You've just got to be humble about it.

THE GOLDEN RULE OF STREAKING

The best streaker is a humble streaker. Streakers should be seen and not heard. Part of the magical allure of the streaker is the "blink and you might miss him" factor. In this way, a successful streaker is a lot like a unicorn. A streaker is also a lot like a unicorn in that they both have phallic protrusions. However, this is only true if the streaker is a male, or a postoperative female-to-male transsexual, or a woman wearing a strap-on. But I digress.

Here's an example of Bad Streaking:

Consider, if you will, "College Joe." He works out regularly and has what some might call a "hot bod." College Joe can often be found shirtless at parties, playing Frisbee on the quad, or just hanging around his dorm room with his best bros. College Joe will tell you that he is shirtless because he is sweaty and wants to cool down or he forgot to put on a shirt.

In truth, College Joe is shirtless because he likes his body and thinks he looks great with no shirt on and/or he wants you to admire his shirtless body.

College Joe carries a plastic cup of beer with him at all times. He wears a LIVESTRONG bracelet and a white baseball cap turned backwards. When College Joe drinks too much alcohol, he is prone to rowdy, aggressive behavior—laughing too loudly, bumping into strangers, getting into fights, and even making inappropriate sexual advances. College Joe also considers himself to be a "rull[12] funny guy." He enjoys playing pranks on all of his school chums, fraternity brothers, and dorm mates. He has committed all of Dane Cook's comedy albums to memory and can recite them at a moment's notice. In short: College Joe is the life of the party.

Now consider College Joe streaking. He is inebriated, calling out lewd remarks and gesticulating wildly with his arms. He says things like, "Look a' my balls!" "Look a' my butt!" "Look a' my balls and butt!" His balls are shaved. His butt is chiseled. His body is tan from head to toe. One suspects that he might wear a "cock ring" from time to time. He looks like a male model on the cover of a fitness magazine or a porn "actor."

When you see College Joe streaking, you experience no joy. Why? College Joe has violated many principles of "Good Streaking Etiquette." *College Joe was not quiet. College Joe was both a good runner and had a good body. College Joe deliberately called attention to himself, thus preventing the "streaker as unicorn" phenomenon.*

Here's an example of Good Streaking:

Consider, if you will, "Shy Michael Showalter." Shy Michael Showalter is a thirty-eight-year-old man who lives in Brooklyn Heights, New York City. He belongs to no fraternity, has few friends, and is a relatively obscure sketch comedian and cat lover. He is hardworking, pleasant, and starting to get a bit fat. He is hardly the life of the party and may even suffer from extreme social awkwardness or Asperger's Syndrome.

---

12. *Rull* is a funny way of saying *real*.

He wears the same sweater every day and he smells like a combination of coffee, grilled cheese sandwiches, and pine needles.

Shy Michael is famous among his friends for his rare but memorable outbursts of silliness. His outbursts are unpredictable and strangely out of character for someone who is normally so shy and reserved. It's refreshing and endearing to see him lose it every once in a while.

One night at a party, Shy Michael has had one too many drinks. For Shy Michael, one too many drinks = fifteen drinks. He acts goofy and people start to wonder what he will do next. Shy Michael disappears into the bathroom and returns wearing only his socks, shoes, a wool hat, a scarf, and a pair of mittens. Other than that, he is completely naked. The very sight of him is funny and maybe kind of sad.

"Let's go for a good ol' fashioned streak around the block!" he yells. And with that, Shy Michael bolts out the door, jogging awkwardly through the quiet, cold night. Everyone dies laughing as they chase after him.

Out on the street, Shy Michael runs silently, except for an occasional yelp. He is not a graceful runner. He looks ridiculous. His noodly wang flops about like a windsock. Several neighbors hear a ruckus outside and open their front doors to see what's going on. When they see Shy Michael loping past them, they can't help but giggle. It is a life-affirming moment for all.

My Morning Routine, #3

I was coming into my building today and saw this flyer taped to the wall next to the elevator:

MOVING SALE!!!!

Sofa BED (Queen size) $50
Love Seat Sofa $300
Baby Bjorn potty $5
Breast Pump (like new) $50
Ceiling Fans 40$ and 30$

So, first of all, why put the dollar in front sometimes and not other times? One of the ceiling fans is ten dollars shittier than the other? It's a love seat AND a sofa? How is that possible?

Breast Pump (like new) $50

Let me repeat: "Breast pump (like new)." My feeling is that with things that you attach to your body and excrete into there's really no such thing as "like new." It's either new or it's not. I mean, you'd never put this sign up in your lobby:

Turkey Sandwich (like new) $7
Jock Strap (like new) $12
Cat Litter (like new) $8

Notice: She didn't tell us that the BabyBjörn potty was "like new," did she? Judging by the price of the BabyBjörn potty, five bucks, I'd say it's hardly new at all. I'd say that BabyBjörn potty has some serious wear and tear on it. Lady, if you're trying to sell a baby toilet for five bucks, maybe you should just throw it away. Do you need the five bucks that badly? But the breast pump is "like new." Okay, so, maybe she only pumped milk out of her breast with it "a few times"? Maybe she only milked herself "sporadically"? I'm not buying it—literally and figuratively. I think this would have been a more appealing pitch:

Working Breast Pump $50 or **Really Great Breast Pump!!!! $50**

By writing "Really Great Breast Pump," she's vouching for it without forcing us to contemplate *why* she knows it's great. It's subliminal advertising. She knows it's great because she's milked herself with it a bunch of times but she doesn't have to say that.

Boy Meets Girl, Boy Buys Three-Piece Suit

The archetypal love story goes: "Boy gets girl, boy loses girl, boy gets girl back." My own experience hasn't exactly followed that formula. I've tried very hard to live my life as if it were a romantic comedy, with rather mixed results. When I was in high school, I did not have much luck with ladies. The girls who I had crushes on had crushes on all my friends. I was the guy they'd come to for advice, to find out if my friends liked them back.

I'm a junior in high school. I'm the last American virgin and I am convinced that the reason girls don't like me is because my nose is too big. I think that the size of my nose has rendered me incapable of kissing. To test my theory, I sneak into the bathroom and practice kissing the mirror. Sure enough, my nose is too big to kiss a mirror. I'm doomed.

I have since learned that human faces are more contoured or "less flat" than a mirror.

I'm a senior in high school and I'm totally in love with a girl named Rosalind. Last night, I gave her a ride home from a student council meeting. When we got to her house, she hesitated for a moment before getting out of the car. Suddenly, I began to hyperventilate, because I could sense that something unusual was going on. It was a dangerous, anything-can-happen sort of feeling.

"Michael, have you ever thought about . . . us?" she asked.

"Um, yeah," I said. My knee was shaking like crazy.

The rest is a blur. We made out a little bit in the car. I drove home in a daze.

A few weeks later, she dumped me over the phone. I was heart-broken. I felt like I was going to die. I went for a long walk, listened to Jane's Addiction on my Walkman, and literally kicked rocks.

I have just finished my freshman year in college, and Rosalind and I both have summer jobs in Princeton. She works at a bakery in town and I work at finding excuses to go to the bakery she works at. We are spending a lot of time together, having coffee and seeing movies.

Last weekend we saw Lethal Weapon *and I impressed her with my analysis about how Mel Gibson and Danny Glover's relationship is a metaphor for gay love. I'm beginning to think that we might start dating again.*

The other night, we were out late talking, and she told me that she was going out of town for the weekend to visit her ex-boyfriend from college. I got a pit in my stomach the size of a beanbag. I asked her if she wanted to get back together with him. She said she didn't know. Fuuuuuuuucccccccckkkkk!

While she's out of town visiting him, my friend Oliver convinces me to "lay it on the line" when she returns. He tells me to "go for it." So I go to the Salvation Army store in Princeton and pick out a scruffy, brown three-piece suit. I also buy her some flowers and write a big, dopey speech professing my feelings for her. Hopefully, she'll take the bait.

Today is the day that she's supposed to come home but she hasn't come home yet. I'm playing it cool. I've called her house every hour or so, but I'm starting to worry.

"Hi, is Rosalind back yet?" I ask.

"No, Michael. I'll have her call you as soon as she gets in."

Then I'll relax for thirty minutes, stress for thirty minutes, then I'll call her again.

I just got off the phone with her mom.

"Hi, is Rosalind back yet?" I asked.

This time there was a long pause.

"Michael," she said, "she's not coming back."

"What?" I asked. I felt that beanbag pit again.

"She's staying for the whole week. She and her ex-boyfriend got back together."

"Thank you," I said, and I hung up. After that I put on my stupid three-piece suit, stole a six-pack out of my parents' fridge, and got drunk.

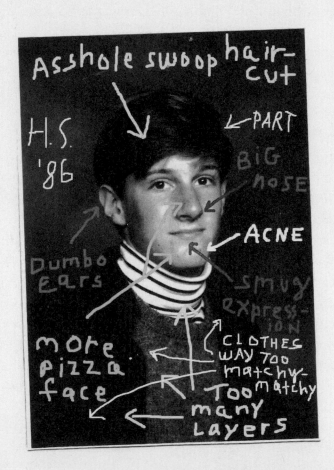

Boy Gets Girl, Boy Goes Out and Buys a Lime Green Futon

It's 9:00 a.m. I am sitting at my computer trying to write about when I got dumped in college:

> *It's my junior year of college, and I have my first "college girlfriend." Her name is Agatha. She's British and sings alto in a coed a cappella group that does a killer four-part harmony rendition of "Benny and the Jets." Her voice is smoky. I've always seen myself dating a smoky-voiced British alto in college. It's meant to be.*

My writing is interrupted by the sound of my actual girlfriend calling to me from our bedroom. "Hey, babe," she says. She sounds groggy. I ignore her and try to keep writing:

> *Agatha and I started dating a week or two before the winter break. We "hooked up" at a party and became inseparable for the next ten days. Over winter break I took home a photograph of her and showed it to all of my friends, proudly proclaiming: "This is my super-serious college girlfriend."*
> *When I get back to school, the entire campus is covered in a blanket of snow. I'm wearing my black wool overcoat and I feel like Holden Caulfield. I can't wait to see Agatha. We've been apart for almost a month, and not a moment passed over break when I wasn't thinking about her.*

"Babe?!!!" my girlfriend yelps. I try one more time to ignore her. "Babe?!" She won't be denied.

"What, honey?" I call back.

"Come here," she says.

"Dammit! I'm working!" I reply.

"You have to see this! Come here!" She's insistent.

"What is it!?"

"Come here now or you'll miss it!" she says.

I know exactly what this is about. She probably wants me to look at one of our cats doing something cute. It's probably Louise sleeping in a funny position. "Okay," I say. "I'm coming."

"Walk softly," she says.

I tiptoe into the bedroom and, sure enough, Louise is sleeping on the bed in a funny position, full body extension, legs sticking out in every direction, head curled under her paw.

"Wow," I say. "That's pretty cute."

"Isn't it?"

"I'm going back to work now."

"Okay. I just wanted you to see."

"Okay," I say. "Thanks." I scuffle back to my computer and get back to the writing:

I call Agatha as soon as I get into my dorm room. I get her voicemail. I leave a message: "Hey, Agatha, it's your boyfriend, Mike. I hope you had a great winter break. I can't wait to see you. I'm sure you'll call as soon as you get in. Take care. Talk soon." She doesn't call back. I figure that maybe she is still in the UK. I mean, I did get here a few days early, so maybe she just hasn't gotten back yet.

Oh God, is there any worse feeling in the world than being blown off? I'd rather get frostbite than be blown off. Truly.

A whole week goes by, and despite my many phone calls, I still haven't heard from her. Radio silence. I've been asking mutual

friends if they've seen her, and they all say things like "Yeah, I
don't know," and "I can't talk now, I'm late for class," and then I'll
say, "What class?" and they'll say, "I know, right?" and then they
scurry off.

I press Save. I look up from the computer and see that my cat Tim is
sleeping in a funny position. He's totally passed out. He's like a lump of
bones. He almost seems dead. It's pretty cute. I call out to my girlfriend:
"Babe?!" She's in the bathroom drying her hair. No reply. "Babe?" I try
again. She's not responding. "Babe?!"

"What?!" she asks. She sounds a bit annoyed.

"Come here!" I say.

"Do I have to?" she says.

"Yes! You have to see this!"

"Really?"

"Yes! Come now or you'll miss it!" I can hear her coming. "Walk
softly," I say. "If you make too much noise, you'll wake him up." She
walks in and looks at Tim sleeping in the cute position. She nods and
goes back into the bathroom to continue drying her hair. I go back to
my story about getting dumped.

I have decided that the reason I haven't heard from Agatha is that
she is upset because my futon is too small. I have a single futon and
it is the lumpiest futon ever. It's like sleeping on a bag of congealed
oatmeal. Whenever she sleeps over, neither of us gets much sleep.
It's really not even big enough for one person, let alone two. I figure
if I get a bigger futon, all will be well.

My train of thought is again interrupted. "Hey, babe!?" I can hear
my girlfriend calling to me from the kitchen. I pretend not to hear her
and continue typing. "Babe?" she calls again. I keep typing. "Babe?!"

I look up from the computer. "Dammit! *What?*"

"Come here, you have to see this!"

"I'm working!" I say,

"Quick! Come now or you'll miss it!"

Now it's probably that our cat Sally is watching her do the dishes. I'm sure of it. Every morning she makes me look at Sally watching her do dishes. "Okay, I'm coming," I say.

"Walk quietly," she says.

I tiptoe into the kitchen and, sure enough, Sally is watching her do the dishes. In fairness: It's cute. I say as much. She thanks me for looking at it. I go back to my computer.

I went into the futon store near campus and walked out the proud owner of a brand-new queen-size, ultra-fluffy, lime green futon.

Later that day, sitting on my new futon still in its plastic casing, I called Agatha to give her the big news. This time she picked up. Oh happy day!

"Agatha, hi!" I say.

"Hi, Michael," she says.

"How are you?" I ask. "We haven't spoken in so long."

"I know," she says. "I've been really busy."

"Yeah," I say. "I can imagine."

I really couldn't imagine, but I tried to be cool about it.

"What've you been up to?" she asks.

"Not much," I say. "How about you?"

"Not much."

"I got a new futon," I say.

"Oh really?" she says. She sounds psyched!

"Yeah. It's a queen-size futon, lime green. I figured that the single futon was too small for us, so I bought us a bigger one."

She's quiet for a minute. Then she speaks.

"Um. Do you mind if I come over?" she asks.

"Not at all," I say. Do I mind? I'm thrilled. I'm overjoyed at the prospect of trying in vain to have sex with her on my new futon. "I can't wait to see you!" I say.

"I'm coming right over," she says and hangs up. Click.

I rip the plastic wrapping off the futon as fast as I can. Her dorm is across the street. She could be here in two minutes. I quickly make the bed and tidy up. "This is great," I'm thinking to myself. "Just great!"

I hear the buzzer. I run to answer the door. She's standing there. She looks fantastic, British, smoky-voiced. We hug. I lead her into my room and show her the new futon. She smiles.

"Here, let's sit down," I say.

"Okay," she says.

We sit on the futon. "Michael, there's something I want to tell you," she says.

"Cool," I say, "but before you say anything, tell me, do you love the futon?"

"Yeah, it's great," she says.

"I got it for us," I say. "So, you were saying?"

She pauses for a really long time, staring at the floor.

I press Save again. I notice that Sally and Louise are play fighting at my feet. "Babe!" I call out to my girlfriend. Now she's in the bedroom getting dressed for work. I get no response. "Babe?" I try again. She's pretending not to hear me. "Babe?!"

"What?" she finally responds.

"You gotta see this!" I say.

"I can't! I'm getting ready for work!" She sounds irritated.

"No! Come now or you'll miss it!"

"Ugh! Fine!" she says. I can hear her scampering in.

Then she says, in a voice almost too quiet to hear, "I just want to be friends."

"Me too," I say, not realizing what's just happened.

"Really?" She seems happy.

"Of course," I say. "Friends, lovers, all of it."

"That's not what I mean," she says.

"Are you breaking up with me?" I say. I'm beginning to piece it all together.

"Yes," she says.

"You're breaking up with me on the new futon that I just bought us?"

"Yes," she says. "I'm really sorry."

"Oh, that's okay," I say. Even though it isn't. "I needed it anyway."

She shakes my hand and leaves.

Cut to: It's 4:00 a.m. I'm sleeping. "Babe?" my girlfriend is whispering to me and nudging me awake. I ignore her. "Babe?" she whispers again. "I'm sleeping," I groan. "You have to see this," she says. All three cats are sleeping in a clump on the bed.

Boy Gets Girl but Then Discovers Girl Already Has Boyfriend

The first time it happened it was with a woman named Sarah.

I'd had a crush on her for a long time. One day we ran into each other on the subway, and, in my mind, we flirted. In her mind, I think we'd only run into each other on the subway. I got her number and asked her to coffee. We met for coffee and on our date, I asked her how she was. She said, "I'm great. My boyfriend and I just got engaged." I nodded and pretended not to care.

Several months later, I met a woman who worked at the coffee shop in Park Slope where I like to write sometimes. She was attractive and seemed smart and funny, so I assumed she had a boyfriend and wrote her off. Then she asked me out to dinner to "talk about comedy." I accepted, considering the possibility that it was just a pick-up line, but I convinced myself not to get my hopes up.

We met for dinner. I picked her up in my car, and we drove to a Pan-Asian restaurant. She was soaked in perfume. During the meal, the word "comedy" did not come up once. I asked her if she had brought with her the script that she'd said she wanted me to look at. She hadn't. I started to think she had ulterior motives. After we finished eating, I asked what she was doing for the rest of the night. Her response: "I'm free until eleven, and then I'm meeting my boyfriend for a drink."

"Oh," I say, as I feel my self-esteem slipping out my asshole.

"Yeah," she says, trying to act like this is no big deal, like we both knew all along that she had a boyfriend and that we were only there to read her skit that she didn't even bring with her because she was too busy getting dressed up and slathering her body in dewberry perfume for our date.

"Maybe we should just wrap it up then?" I say.

She thinks for a bit, then says, "Yeah. I think that would be best."

"I think that would be best?" Like I had done something inappropriate! What she really meant was: "I understand this situation completely and agree with you that us hanging out for another hour is a bad idea because I have a boyfriend and you want to *be* my boyfriend, but I don't want you to be my boyfriend because I really like the boyfriend I already have, and I just wanted to talk to you about the skit that I didn't even bring with me."

We shake hands outside the restaurant. I'm trying to keep up a good face, but I know it's not working. I'm visibly destroyed, and she knows it. I wish her well and drive home. As I drive, I feel like I'm in a Radiohead video. It's cold and drizzling, and all I can hear is the sound of my windshield wipers swooshing back and forth. It's a lonely feeling. It's an "I need to either write poetry or slit my throat" feeling.

One week later, I'm sitting on a park bench with my notebook and pen. I'm pretending to be writing this book, but there's this young woman sitting on a stoop across the street with her dog, and she's staring at me. I'm wearing my classic Ray-Bans ($200), so she can't tell that I'm staring back. From the looks of her, I'd say she's probably twenty-seven or twenty-eight years old. She's attractive but in an "I don't know that I'm attractive but I actually do" sort of way. She has curly dark brown hair, and she's wearing a flowery dress. Stop this! Write, Michael! Boxers box! The journey's the reward! I write:

Shoes are funny. It's funny to me that we could be so advanced in so many ways, like we can split atoms and communicate over the Internet and cure all sorts of illnesses, but every morning after we wake up, we put a protective wrapping around our feet, and we call this wrapping shooze.

I look up from my notebook, and the woman is walking over to me with her dog. Maybe she's just walking toward the park. Maybe this is all in my imagination. Maybe she just wants to walk her dog in the park. It really feels like she's walking directly toward me, though.

"Hi," she says.

She is. She was.

"Hi," I say as I close up my notebook. I don't want her to see my "shoes" bit.

"Are you Michael?" she says.

"Yes," I say.

She establishes that we have a friend in common. It's a guy named Mattieu who, truthfully, I'm not sure I actually know, but it doesn't matter. We talk. She's twenty-three, a Wesleyan grad, and an aspiring actress with an interest in comedy. She seems very smart and funny. I can tell we have a lot in common. We exchange email addresses. I'm a bit too nervous to keep talking, so I pretend that I have somewhere to be, and we go our separate ways. The minute I get home, I write her an email. It reads:

Dear Abigail,

It was really nice to meet you today at the park in Cobble Hill. I wondered if you'd like to go on a date with me sometime? Perhaps get a cup of coffee or grab a bite? I hate to be blunt, but just to be clear, I am asking you on a date. If you have a boyfriend already, please tell me now because the last time I went on a date I took her to a Pan-Asian restaurant and she waited until the end of the meal to tell me that she had a boyfriend and it really sucked. Once bitten, twice shy, I suppose. I hope that's not a really weird thing to say. Again, it was nice to meet you. I hope that all is well.

Best,
Michael

Later that night, she responds:

Dear Michael,
    I would love to go on a date with you. Coffee sounds great! I am
free most afternoons. What works for you?
    Best,
    Abigail

I'm thinking, "Thank God! What a breath of fresh air!" I felt so stung by my last dating experience that, regardless of the outcome, it's a huge relief not to have so much ambiguity.

We make a plan to have coffee later that week. She has a day job working at a little pastry shop in Cobble Hill, and I meet her at four when her shift ends. We walk down Court Street past Atlantic Avenue into Brooklyn Heights. She's never seen the Brooklyn Promenade before. We hit it off. We laugh. She tells me she's got a boyfriend. To repeat: *We hit it off. We laugh. She tells me she's got a boyfriend.*

Dos and Don'ts for Girls with Boyfriends Who Go Out on Dates with Guys Who Aren't Their Boyfriends

(aka "Dos and Don'ts for Girls with Boyfriends Who Went Out on Dates with Me and Didn't Tell Me They Had Boyfriends Until I'd Already Gotten My Hopes up for a Relationship with Them")

• *DO* tell him before the date that you have a boyfriend. You never know what his intentions are, and, among adults, it is always good to be up-front.

• *DON'T* wait until he's gotten all dressed up in a charcoal-grey ragg wool turtleneck sweater that he bought specifically for the date because his other sweaters were covered in cat hair and Ritz Cracker crumbs, and driven all the way across town to pick you up in his car that he cleaned all the empty paper coffee cups and newspapers out of and took to the car wash earlier that day so you'd think he was husband material, and taken you out to a nice Pan-Asian restaurant, expressed genuine interest in you and your "outreach work," and gotten his hopes up that there'd be a serious make out session later on, and asked you at the end of the meal what you were doing for the rest of the night, and you say "nothing," he says, "great," and then you say, "I'm totally free until eleven, when I have to go meet my boyfriend." Don't wait that long.

- DO understand that men find you attractive and that they don't want to be your "buddy," they want to be your boyfriend. (In fairness to men, it's not purely sexual, they genuinely want to get to know you too, but chomping your box is part of that.)

- DON'T assume things. When his email to you says: "I am asking you on a date. If you have a boyfriend, please tell me because I took my last date to a Pan-Asian restaurant, and she told me after the meal that she had a boyfriend and it kinda sucked," don't assume that what he actually means is "I just want to be your buddy."

- DON'T flirt with him shamelessly if you have a boyfriend.

- DO not flirt with him shamelessly if you have a boyfriend.

- DO leave him alone after you've broken his heart by telling him that you have a boyfriend, which is something that he didn't realize until it was way too late, because you decided that wasn't an important detail, even though he specifically said, "If you have a boyfriend, please tell me because I took my last date to a Pan-Asian restaurant, and she told me after the meal that she had a boyfriend and it kinda sucked." Give him his much-needed space to heal his wounded pride.

- DON'T send him text messages all the time bemoaning the fact that you can't be friends. He doesn't want to be your friend. He wants to be your lover, and if he can't be your lover, then he wants nothing to do with you. Why? Because he's an adult, and he's not looking for friends! He's looking for someone to fuck, to be fucked by, and to watch CNN with.

• *DO* move to another country after you humiliate him at the end of the date by telling him that you have a boyfriend. If you can't think of a country to move to, I have a few suggestions. In no particular order: Poland, Antarctica, Ancient Egypt.

• *DON'T* call him up and invite him places with you and your boyfriend. You don't seem to grasp the fact that he is *not* your "buddy" and he never will be. If you really want to know the truth, he utterly despises the idea of being your "buddy" and would rather be dead than hang out at some shitty *tapas* restaurant with you and your douche bag copywriter boyfriend from Ohio who has too many freckles and smells like a box of raisins.

Bad Advice to Guys for When They Take a Lady Out on a Date

When you and your date sit down to eat, briskly take the menu away from her and insist on ordering for both of you. By "briskly" I'm more saying aggressively *snatch it* out of her hands. Then say, "If you don't mind, girlfriend, I'll just order for the two of us. I'm a foodie." Then throw out a few foodie terms: *gastrique, twice porked, lemon salt.*

Now, menu in hand, order her *the gamiest-sounding thing on the menu*. If you're not sure what's gamey on the menu just ask the waiter, "Waiter, what's your most heavily meated entree?" After you've ordered her a ton of gravy-drenched beef or fowl, then order yourself a *tiny salad*. See, women love eating big, disgusting plates of very strongly flavored meat, and they particularly love eating big plates of strongly flavored meat if their date's only eating a small salad. Buddy—you're halfway home!

Before the food comes, place the napkin in your shirt like a bib. No, not *place* the napkin in your shirt, *stuff* the napkin in your shirt. Once your food arrives, be sure to get tons of food on it. And once or twice during the meal use the napkin to blow your nose. Be certain to really dig the napkin into your nostril. Dig so hard that your nostril moves around a lot while you're shoving the napkin in your nose. Like, really manipulate the cartilage.

During the meal: Talk *only* about yourself; brag about your achievements; insult people more successful than you; come across as bitter and resentful of others; *don't ask her any questions about herself.* If you're depressed, then by all means *tell her.* Tell her about all of your insecurities! Really bare your soul and don't be afraid to appear *very weak*! If you're unhappy or unfulfilled in your life, or shitty in bed, *tell her about this.* She will really appreciate it. And when she begins talking, *immediately* interrupt her and change the subject. And I mean like *really* interrupt her. Cut her off mid-sentence.

When her meal arrives, touch her food to make sure it's the right temperature. Do this with her water as well. Make sure it's cold. Don't be shy. Use your whole hand: your palm, your thumb, knuckles. Really touch it with your hand.

Excuse yourself at some point and say, "Will you pardon me for a sec, I gotta take a big ol' dump." (Don't leave out the *ol'*, that's key. If you don't say *ol'*, it will seem crass. By putting the *ol'* in, it will seem old-fashioned in a good way.) Take a long time in the bathroom. When you return, say something like, "Wow. I just lost thirty pounds in there!" If that doesn't totally crack her up, then you might be in for a long night. But I'm telling you. It will crack her up. It's a really funny joke.

When the check comes, take out your library card, give it to the waiter, and say, "This should just about cover it." When the waiter brings the card back and says that it's not a valid form of payment, apologize to him and your date. Then take out your CVS discount card and give that to the waiter. Say, "This oughta do the trick." When he returns again, you should act frustrated and ask your date if she can pay the bill. You should be very apologetic. Ultimately, you will have shown her that you (a) go to the library and (b) go to CVS. Women like a man who reads books and buys toothpaste.

If you don't want to do the library card gambit, then say, "I believe in Women's Lib and insist that we go dutch." She will be impressed that you area a "modern man." After the meal, when the check comes, take out a calculator and figure out exactly what each of you owes. She will see that you are organized and "good about money."

Finally, grab a very big handful of mints on your way out and stuff them in your pocket. Tell her, "You never know when these will come in handy." Insist on not walking her home. Tell her that you believe that "chivalry is dead." Tell her that you have "somewhere else to be." You don't want her to think you have no life.

Now, let's assume the date goes well and the two of you begin to see each other more regularly. At a certain point she will say to you, "I can only pretend for our first seven dates that I don't shit. On our next date, I will, in all likelihood, have to take a shit. I hope you can handle that." Of course you'll call her bluff. She's lying. Women don't do that. They can't. They don't have colons.

Now listen, you might want to tell her, "Remember on our first date when I told you that *The Secret Life of Bees* was *my* favorite book *too*? That was a lie. I've kind of heard of it, I guess, but I don't know what it's about." She'll really appreciate your honesty, and even though you haven't told her that you're not British yet, I predict she'll forgive you. You were cursed with the ability to do an amazing British accent. It's getting you laid but the charade can't go on forever.

You also might want to tell her, "Remember when I let you use my computer and you saw that I had a link on my toolbar for a penis enlargement website and I told you that I was using it for research on a college paper that I was writing about penis enlargement websites and then you said, 'But you're not in college, you're in your thirties. Why would you be writing papers?' And then I suddenly had that asthma attack and then the subject got changed to my asthma attack and then the penis enlargement website conversation kind of got swept under the rug? Well, the truth is that I don't have asthma and I'm not writing a paper on penis enlargement websites. The truth is that I am being paid by the CIA to test these supplements because many of these so-called penis enlargement websites are actually just fronts for Taliban propaganda." This will really move the relationship forward.

Here's a common problem: If she snores and it bothers you, don't say, "You snored last night." This might offend her. Instead say, "Good morning, honey. Oh by the way, was I *also* snoring last night?" This is a much more inclusive way of telling her that she sounds like a moose eating granola when she sleeps. She will probably say, "No. You weren't.

Why? I was snoring?" And then you say, "Yeah, I guess, but I was more wondering if I was snoring too." Keep it focused on yourself.

Now let's say that she dumps you because, well, you're a horrible person. You're wondering if you're heartbroken about it but you don't know because you aren't in touch with your feelings. Well, here're some signs that you're upset about it.

Uncontrollable bouts of crying

Assuming fetal position in shower

Inability to enjoy things you once enjoyed (e.g., eating food, company of friends, breathing air, etc.)

Sudden affinity for music without lyrics

Look, there is nothing more brutal than breaking up and there are no simple solutions. It hurts. It hurts and there's nothing you can do about it. However, if you're really struggling, I do have a few suggestions for how to get over the relationship as quickly as possible.

Have your memory erased. This is not an easy procedure and to my knowledge it's actually not really a procedure at all. That said, if you can do it—do it. Nothing will help you move on more quickly than to have your entire memory erased. Granted, there are pitfalls: You won't know who you are anymore. Then again, did you ever really know who you were? Did you really like antiquing? Or did you just do it because she did? Did you really like Norah Jones? Or were you just saying that?

Move to a foreign country. Again, not easy. I hear that they have excellent universal health care in Denmark. Just a thought. Some might say: "Wherever I go, there I am." But some might also say, "Wherever I go, I get to distract myself from myself for at least a few months before the startling reality of my own misery hits me and then I can just move again." I hear that Costa Rica has beautiful beaches.

Here's one: Get a lobotomy. Extreme? Yes. Effective? Very. Good news: You will no longer feel the daily heartbreak of the breakup. Bad news: You'll be a vegetable. (Hopefully you'll be a cool vegetable, though, like celery root or bok choy. If you're a crappy vegetable like eggplant or turnip, that would suck.)

Why not get frozen in ice? This way you can emerge from the ice a few hundred years from now and she won't even be alive anymore. She'll be dead! Long dead. You couldn't get back together with her even if you tried. She died years ago from old age, her husband at her side. He loved her and she loved him back, and they were rich and happy and had many, many children because they loved having so much sex with each other but also because they loved building a family and they had many grandchildren too, all of whom were well-adjusted and attended either Ivy League schools or at least really good schools as good as Ivy League schools, like Duke and Stanford. Some of the grandkids were musicians and went to conservatories. Obviously you will need to adjust to the new society because you'll be living in the future—and you're now viewed as a FREAK—but at least you're not sad about the breakup anymore.

Perhaps you could join a cult and get brainwashed. Again, all of these suggestions have an upside and a downside. The upside of joining a cult is that your attention will be diverted away from how you're feeling about being dumped; the downside of joining a cult is that you will have joined a cult.

Online University

I recently received this email advertising an online university degree: "Want the degree but can't find the time? We provide a concept that will allow anyone with sufficient work experience to obtain a fully verifiable University Degree: Bachelor's, Master's or even a Doctorate. Think of it, within four to six weeks, you too could be a college graduate. Call us today and give your work experience the chance to earn you the higher compensation you deserve!"

I like the fact that they say "four to six weeks." It's like they're saying, "Hopefully it will only take only four weeks, but we're not going to try to snow job you. Depending on the course load, there is a real chance that it might take six." It gives their program legitimacy. I'll bet that some online universities will promise the degree in four weeks flat. But not this one, they're not in the bullshit business. They're saying, "If you want an ironclad promise that your degree will only take a month, then we're not the school for you, because we can't guarantee that. The simple fact of the matter is that some of our degrees might take fourteen days—or ten working days—longer." But listen, nobody ever said that graduate school was easy. My guess is that if you only want a bachelor's degree, it'll take you four weeks. But if you really want to strive and you have time to really dedicate yourself to an advanced degree, then you'll probably need to matriculate for one extra week, or five business days, to obtain the master's, and two extra weeks, or ten business days, for the doctorate. Because that's the reality of it: If you want the advanced degrees, you need to be mentally prepared to stay in school for a few weeks longer than some of your classmates. It's an enormous drag, yes, but you'll look back on it one day and say, "I'm really glad that I stayed in school those fourteen extra days and got my PhD."

Television Commercial Proposal for Online University

Graphic: "ONLINE UNIVERSITY, FOUNDED IN 2004"

We see ROB BINSON, forties, wearing a toupee. He stands in a room filled with computers.

ROB: Hi, I'm Rob Binson and I'm the president and founder of Online University. Wanna get a PhD in something? Well, if you've got even a modicum of free time, you can get one at Online University for only ten dollars! All you have to do is answer a few yes or no questions and that degree can be yours! Questions like: Are cats cute? Yes or No? Do you like cake? Yes or No? Are you answering these questions? Yes or No? Online University is fast, easy, and totally illegal. But don't take it from me—take it from people who've graduated!

INT. BEDROOM—DAY

A TEENAGE BOY in his bedroom.

TEENAGE BOY: Online University is great because I can learn about Greek poetry and whack off to porn all at the same time!

INT. KITCHEN—DAY

A SOCCER MOM sits in her kitchen. Behind her on the walls are hundreds of framed diplomas.

SOCCER MOM: I'm a housewife with lots of downtime. Through Online University, I managed to get over ninety-seven master of arts degrees in less than two hours! Thanks, Online University!

INT. DOCTOR'S OFFICE—DAY

DOCTOR BOB sits with his patient, who has an arm stitched to his forehead.

DOCTOR BOB: Through Online University, I was able to go to med school in one day. Now I'm a surgeon with my own medical practice.

INT. COMPUTER ROOM

Back to ROB BINSON.

ROB: But OU isn't just about academics. Online University also has a Division III soccer team.

EXT. SOCCER FIELD—DAY

A normal college soccer team dribbles and passes the ball around the field. They maneuver around a bunch of LAPTOP COMPUTERS. The scoreboard reads HALSTON COLLEGE: 30, ONLINE UNIVERSITY: 4.

INT. COMPUTER ROOM

ROB: We also have a brand-new amphitheater, where every year the Online University Theater Department performs a classic American musical. This year they did *Oklahoma*.

INT. THEATER—NIGHT

On the stage we see the curtains open. Music plays. We see a STAGEHAND push a few laptops onto the stage. The laptops all have on COWBOY HATS. A tumbleweed rolls past them. Nothing else happens.

INT. COMPUTER ROOM

ROB: Give us a try! Our admissions offices are located in the back of my car in the parking lot behind the Motel 5 off Route 80 in Acheson, Oklahoma.

Sweaters, Sandwiches, Cats

I have started making lists of things to write about. I looked at my writer's mantra pinned over my desk: "Write What You Know." I asked myself, what *do* I know?

I know that I like sweaters.
I know that I don't like jogging.
I know that I like sandwiches.
I know that I love my cats.

Then I rewrote the list, adding "for a fact" for emphasis.

I know **for a fact** that I like sweaters.
I know **for a fact** that I don't like jogging.
I know **for a fact** that I like sandwiches.
I know **for a fact** that I love my cats.

Okay! Big question: Is this enough for a book? I am skeptical. I think I could probably write for half a page about how I don't like jogging and I think I can squeeze three pages out on sweaters and maybe another three pages on cats. ½ page on jogging + 3 pages on sweaters + 3 pages on cats = 7. (I round up.) That brings me to seven pages tops, plus my quotes page and my thank-you page is nine pages. 1200 pages − 9 pages = 1100 pages. I'm fucked.

1½ Pages on I Hate Jogging Because...

I hate jogging because it looks stupid. No, let me correct myself. I look stupid. I look like a big zucchini with legs. No, worse than zucchini. I look like *zucchini bread* with legs. There, I said it! I admit that when I jog I look like a giant piece of zucchini bread with human legs sticking out of it! Do you know how horrible that is for me? Pretty horrible, let me tell you. And I'm not even talking about the fact that everyone wants to wrap me up in plastic sticky wrap and take me to a dinner party and be all like, "Here, Margot! We made you a zucchini bread." And then Margot's like, "Great! Ezra will be thrilled! He loves zucchini bread." And then they'll be like, "How is Ezra anyway? Is he still working on that Walt Whitman biography?" And then Margot's like, "Here, come into the kitchen. Let me put the zucchini bread in the oven and I'll tell you all about it."

I hate jogging because it's fucked up. It's fucked up because lots of times marathon runners—who jog, no one would argue that—lose control of their bowl (sp?) movements near the end of the race and then they start wobbling and then they poop down their legs and that's fucked up. I mean, it's great that they won a marathon but was it worth hobbling around with poop streaming down their legs? For me, the answer is no. For me, I'd rather not run the marathon. I'd rather stay in that day, eat a sandwich, maybe a bowl of soup, some potato chips, watch TV (maybe even watch the marathon) and in so doing avoid *both* running the marathon (risking hypothermia) but more importantly

I'd avoid *winning the marathon*—which would be an achievement, yes—though I can't say what the prize money would be—and all at the expense of having had everyone see me hobbling to the finish line with bowl (sp?) movements streaming down my legs.

My thing is that jogging feels weird. You know? It feels weird to have my skin and muscle tissue moving up and down on my frame. It's like I'm a pulled pork sandwich. Who wants to *ever* feel like a pulled pork sandwich? Well, fine, obviously if you're in the mood for barbeque, you'll say, "I feel like a pulled pork sandwich." But you don't actually mean that. What you mean to say is, "I'm craving a pulled pork sandwich." Civilization has mutilated the phrase "I feel like." Point being, I don't personally want to ever *feel like* a pulled pork sandwich.

And let's be honest, jogging is bad for you. I already mentioned the part about the pooping on the leg, but it also gets your *heart rate pumping* and that could make you have a heart attack. I don't want that. That's why I smoke! The last thing I want is to be running the last few miles of a marathon, with crud streaming down my leg, then suddenly I have a heart attack, all because I decide to run instead of walk at a clip. To say nothing of the fact that I look like zucchini bread and feel like pulled pork. It's not a good scene.

Lastly, there is the "windsock factor." One's wiener flaps around like a windsock. And I'm assuming that the same could be said for one's boobs. *So in conclusion,* running is bad for you; it makes you poop on your own leg; zucchini bread, feel like pulled pork sandwich, windsock, one's own boobs. Better to walk at a clip.

Sweater Letter

I recently did a stand-up comedy show at a popular bar/club in Brooklyn. Before my set, I took off my sweater and placed it on a chair near the stage. When I came offstage the sweater was gone. I was heartbroken.

Dear person who stole my sweater last week,

My name is Michael Showalter. In my free time I love to cook food for my friends—I make a famous vegetarian lasagna; the secret ingredient is lemon salt. My favorite color is magenta (it's like "magic + polenta") and my favorite book is Old Yeller. *I tell you these things because I want to put a face on that charcoal-grey ragg wool turtleneck sweater that you now own.*

Have you washed it yet? Do you know that it needs to be dry-cleaned, otherwise it will shrink? Have you hung it in your closet? You probably don't know that if you do that, you'll stretch it out and it will lose its shape.

Let me cut to the chase: I am going to give you two options. (1) You can return the sweater to me. No questions asked. Both of our lives can proceed as though none of this ever happened. We might even be friends one day. (2) You can hide like a coward and keep the sweater. Should you choose the second option, please know that I will hunt you down like a dog. You will never be able to go into another coffee shop, used record store, or dive bar again without wondering if I am waiting there for you, lurking in the shadows next to the jukebox. I will strike fast and without warning. One minute you will be on the subway quietly reading a book and the next minute you will notice that your heart has been ripped out of your chest and is rolling down the floor of the subway car. And where your heart used to be will be a Post-it note with this message written on it: "Why?" And you will be asking yourself exactly the same question. But it won't matter because you don't have a heart anymore and before you even have time to reflect on everything you'll be dead. The ball is in your court now. Peace out.

Sincerely,

Michael Showalter

Ps. If you're a girl and not a guy, then I'm much less pissed about the whole thing. Let's hang out.

My Morning Routine, #4

The saying goes, "Six of one, half dozen of the other." But what if it's a baker's dozen? Then what? Are we screwed?

A hospice for frogs is called a frogspice.

Does guinea pig bacon taste like normal bacon? How many pieces of guinea pig bacon would one need to feel full? Would "guinea pigs in a blanket" be a good appetizer?

With Justin Timberlake's solo career up and running, the remaining members of 'N Sync have formed a new group called Band of Roving Losebags.

Would it be weird if cats were as small as mice?

Do lady ogres have a vagina?

A FOR SALE BY OWNER sign is way better than a FOR SALE BY THIEF sign.

I think that Los Angeles smells like an old couch that's been fucked on. It's kind of gross but kind of cool at the same time.

Would there be a riot at an Indigo Girls concert if they decided not to play "Closer to Fine"?

Let's say I ask you, "On a scale from 1 to 10 how much do I love this song?" And you know I really love the song and you say, "Eleven." The reality is that, even though your intention was correct, it's actually as wrong as if you'd said "one." Because, while in theory you were right, technically it's incorrect.

Cats

In my perfect world order, it is cold all the time. Everyone wears sweaters and drinks coffee. People don't speak to each other; they read the newspaper. There is no loud music, and cats are in charge.

I like cats because they are wild and domestic at the same time. One minute they will be cuddling with you or playing with a piece of yarn that you're dangling in front of their nose, and the next minute they will be blowing you off completely and acting as if they've never met you before. I'm like that too.

I had my first cat the year after I graduated from college. I met a Shakespearean actress named Clea at a party in New York City. I overheard her telling people that she had gotten an acting job doing a play in Chapel Hill, North Carolina, and asking whether anyone would cat sit for her while she was gone. I tapped her on the shoulder and said that I would do it. I figured that if I took care of her cat, maybe she'd sleep with me one day.

The next morning, she delivered a moody black cat with white paws, a white scruff, and a white beard. He was a young adult at the time, not quite a kitten, but not quite a full-grown cat either. He was rail thin and very tall when stretched out. Her name for him was Lestat, as in the vampire Lestat from the Anne Rice book *Interview with the Vampire*. She thanked me with a handshake, making it clear that my "sex for cat sitting" ploy would fail, and ran off.

Lestat and I kept our distance that day. Every once in a while he'd glare at me or scratch something to get my attention. He seemed to have emotional issues. I liked him instantly, but I didn't want to seem too eager.

As the days passed into weeks, we warmed to one another. I did, however, struggle with his name, and he didn't seem to like it much either. It was a problematic name.

For one thing, *Lestat* was very difficult to pronounce. *Stat* in particular does not roll off the tongue. It's a harsh syllable. Also, most people did not know what it meant, or what it referred to, and explaining it was tiresome. Most of all, speaking plainly, it was a bad name.

I decided that if I was going to be this cat's roommate for a few months, I would need to change his name. I didn't want to confuse him by changing it entirely. I wanted to preserve the essence of the name, but I also wanted him to have a great new "non-awful" name. The moniker I devised was "Lester." I "Ellis Islanded" him, and I'm quite certain he liked *Lester* more than *Lestat*.

Lester and I grew closer. Months passed and Clea was set to return from North Carolina. I waited to hear from her, but she never called. Clea, to my knowledge, never returned from North Carolina. Lester and I spent the next fourteen years together.

One day, I came home and found him lying underneath my coffee table in a very awkward position. It seemed odd to me, because he never slept underneath the coffee table, and I'd also never seen him in this particular position before. I took him to the vet. They told me that something was wrong with his liver, and he was hospitalized for a week. After that, he was fine for eight months, but then it happened again, and he spent another week at the vet. The telltale signs were always the same: He'd be lying in a spot he'd never lain down in before and he'd always be sprawled out in that same uncomfortable pose. It happened again in five months, then three months, and so on. I kept him going as long as I could.

The last year of his life, my roommate Andrea and I had to hydrate him intravenously every day. He had lost so much weight that he started to look like the kitten version of himself I had never met.

One day, I came home, and I could see that he needed to go to the vet again. This time, I could see in his eyes that he didn't feel like coming home. I called Andrea and she met us at the vet. Lester had fought too long and was ready to move on. We took him into the small doctor's office and laid him down on the table. He was purring. The doctor filled a syringe with blue liquid and slowly injected it into Lester's leg. I held him in my arms. He was purring the whole time. And then he was gone.

I haven't been able to get a new cat since. This year, though, I decided that I was ready. I found myself looking in pet shop windows. I was looking for two cats, not kittens but not adult cats either, a boy and a girl. A friend recommended the big PETCO in Union Square. They have a room filled with cats up for adoption. Whenever I was in the city, I'd pop into PETCO to see who was there. All the cats were wonderful, but I was looking for a boy and a girl who knew each other. They were proving hard to come by.

One afternoon, I stopped in PETCO and found exactly what I was looking for, two young cats, a brother and sister. I tried to get the attention of one of the store workers, but they were all very busy trying to look busy, and none of them seemed to want to help me. All of the men and women who work in the cats section at PETCO have that "angry vegan" vibe, like if they think you own a TV, they won't talk to you. I found this frustrating but felt that I could deal with the lameness of their service for the sake of the cats. Finally, one of them, a woman in an Ani DiFranco concert T-shirt, very impatiently answered my question.

"Hi, I'd like to adopt these cats. How do I do that?" I said.

"You have to come back at six o'clock and talk to one of the adoption reps." She answered my question, sighed, judged me, scoffed at me, and rolled her eyes all at the same time, which I thought was an impressive feat of cuntiness.

The idea of having to come back at six o'clock to adopt the cats seemed odd to me. I assumed that they would be eager to move the cats out of there. Still, I really felt like these cats were cute, so I agreed to return at six.

Six o'clock arrived, and I showed up on time. Again, I found it difficult to get anyone's attention, but finally a very harried woman wearing bifocals on a string around her neck and a gigantic sweater that looked like it was a thousand years old and made out of bark agreed to talk to me. I told her that I wanted to adopt the cats. She groaned and handed me a questionnaire to fill out. It asked basic questions like address, phone number, and email. I filled it out, handed it back to her, and then she asked me if I would "sit down for an interview."

"An interview?" I said, incredulous.

"Yes," she said. "It's standard that we interview prospective owners."

"Okay," I said. I was truly flummoxed. I felt like I was applying for a bank loan. Where I come from, getting a cat is easier than buying a pair of socks.

She pulled up two chairs. She took out a pencil and a clipboard. She took meticulous notes as I answered her questions.

"How big is your apartment?" she asked.

"You mean square footage?"

"Yes," she said.

"I don't really know," I said, "but it's pretty big."

She raised an eyebrow and made a note of it: *"Doesn't know size of apartment."*

"What about your windows?" she asked.

"What about them?"

"Do they have screens?" she asked.

"I think so," I said. "If they don't, I'll get them."

She made another note: *"Isn't sure if windows have screens."*

"How much money do you make annually?" she asked.

"You're joking, right?"

"Not at all," she said.

"It depends," I said.

"On what?" she asked.

"On what I make," I said.

She winced and scribbled down more notes: *"Depends on what he makes."*

"And what kind of food do you feed your cats?"

"I don't have any cats," I said. "That's why I'm here."

"What kind of food *will* you feed your cats?"

"Cat food." I was losing patience.

"What kind of cat food?" So was she.

"I don't know. What's the good kind?" I didn't want to say the wrong thing.

She scribbled, *"Didn't state type of food would feed cats."*

She asked me a few more intrusive questions and told me that I'd be hearing from "them." I thanked her sarcastically and scuttled off. In truth, I had answered all her questions as fairly as I could. After all, I was trying to adopt stray cats from "them." Should that be difficult? I know I'm a doting pet owner. I felt that I had nothing to prove.

The following week, I received a phone call from "them." This time, I was speaking to a man named "Mickey." Even though I put the name "Mickey" in quotation marks, that's his real name. Mickey asked me if I would come back to PETCO for a second interview.

I could tolerate the first interview, but this was fucked up. I asked him why. He said that there were a few more questions they'd like to ask. At this point, it was getting personal. I said I would be there that night. I canceled my evening plans and returned to PETCO at six p.m. to meet with "Mickey" (his real name).

When I arrived, "they" were all there—the woman in the sweater made out of bark, the girl in the Ani DiFranco T-shirt, and Mickey. Mickey was the ringleader. Mickey was a small little man in his forties. He had a tiny little Hitler mustache, tiny little hands, and a tiny little sweater that he wore over his tiny little shirt that was tucked into his tiny little pants. Mickey brought me over to the chairs, and we resumed our interview.

"How old was your last cat when he died?" he asked.

"Pretty old," I said.

"How old?" he asked.

"I don't know," I said. "Maybe fourteen or fifteen?"

Mickey raised his little eyebrows and said, "That's not so old."

He quickly scribbled something down. This time I couldn't read it. We spoke for a few more minutes and then it was over.

"You'll be hearing from us," he said as he scuffled off.

"Thanks, Mickey," I said, but he didn't hear me. He was gone.

A few days later, I received a letter from the cat adoption center at PETCO. Here's what it said:

> *Dear Maribel,*
>
> *Thank you for your application and taking the time to be interviewed at KittyKats. As discussed by the adoption rep, an application is not a guarantee of adoption. The selection criteria for adoption incorporate many aspects, and your application was not approved, as it did not meet KittyKats criteria.*
>
> *Sincerely,*
>
> *KittyKats*

THE LETTER I WISH I'D WRITTEN THEM BACK:

> *Dear Cat Adoption Selection Committee,*
>
> *Let's just get a few things straight. First and foremost, my name is not Maribel. My name is Michael. Whereas I can easily see how you would have gotten my name wrong considering that Michael and Maribel both start with the letter M, to have rejected my application for a cat while simultaneously mocking me by calling me girly names just seemed like kind of a low blow.*
>
> *In the spirit of full disclosure, I like the name Maribel. I could have named the girl cat I wanted to adopt from you Maribel, but apparently I'm not qualified to take her out of the small cage you keep her in and give her a big loving home. But it's cool. I totally understand. You guys have a job to do, and let me be the first to say that you're doing your jobs well. And by "well," I actually mean, "NOT WELL."*
>
> *I had no idea that this would be so difficult. I had envisioned something along the lines of, "Hey. I want a cat." And then you'd*

say, "Cool." And then you'd hand me a cat and I'd be out the door. Boy, was I wrong.

Looking back, I'm wondering. Maybe my apartment was too big? Maybe I loved my last cat too much and you thought me to have codependency issues? Or maybe, just maybe, you're just a huge dick.

In conclusion, I hope that all of the cats that you assholes hoard like small children hoarding candy on Halloween are finding homes that do meet your criteria, because criteria sort of rhymes with diarrhea, and diarrhea is what you remind me of.

Sincerely,

Michael Showalter

Cats and Ancient Egypt

People say they don't like cats because they're aloof. I agree that they're aloof, but this is precisely why I like them. It's why I like rich people. Rich people are aloof and don't engage you in small talk. Neither do cats. This is partly because cats don't have language, but also because cats aren't like that. They are more into a substantive debate or no debate at all.

Ancient Egyptians loved them too. (Cats, not rich people.) They liked them because they were good at killing snakes and rats. I like them because they act funny and are soft (cats, not Ancient Egyptians).

People say that dogs are better than cats. I've never seen it as a competition. Why does society force us to take sides on this issue? It's like a Tarantino movie where Michael Madsen has a gun to your head, and he's saying, "Pick one! Cats or dogs! Fucking pick one or I'll blow your fucking brains out!" I'm going to say something very controversial. I like cats *and* dogs. I think that they're both great. I just prefer cats because they're weirder.

Look, dogs probably are smarter than cats. So what? Keith Richards is practically brain-dead, but he's a great musician. Intelligence is a very subjective concept. Truthfully, some of the smartest people I know are intolerable assholes.

The Ancient Egyptians believed that intelligence was stored in the heart. They regarded the brain as that "stuff" inside your head. Kinda like fluffernutter. They believed that the brain did not have any real purpose. Nowadays, people feel that way about Scott Baio, that he has no purpose. Back then, no one even knew who Scott Baio was, let alone what the brain was capable of. Ancient Egyptians had such little regard for the brain that they scooped it out of the skull during mummification like the seeds inside a pumpkin. It was of no importance to them. That's probably why mummies are so dumb. If the Egyptians had left the mummies' brains in, who knows what kind of amazing things the mummies could've accomplished?

First of all, they'd have been able to keep their wrapping on better. Who's going to hire a mummy if his wrapping is hanging off his corpse all willy-nilly? If I'm interviewing a prospective employee and he walks in with wrapping hanging all over his rotting corpse, then I guarantee that's going to be one short interview.

This is of course assuming that mummies are even seeking employment—which, last I checked, they aren't. Equally true is that I'm not hiring anyone right now. But there's an even better reason why mummies aren't seeking employment. It's because they have no brains. What ad agency is going to hire some mummy with no brain? To be honest, I'd be surprised if an ad agency hired a mummy under any circumstances, but with no brain it's almost a fait accompli. Granted, I wrote that last sentence primarily as an excuse to say "fait accompli."

Also, if the mummies had their brains they might be more articulate. Not that I'm expecting them to be spoken word artists or anything but enough with the grunting already. Seriously, mummies! Can't you string three words together and make a sentence? Look, I get it—you're a mummy. You've been buried in a tomb. Big deal, we all have our crosses to bear. I got my ass kicked in fifth grade. Does that mean I have to grunt and moan for the rest of my life? Of course it doesn't. It's not like you're the first person who ever had a shitty day.

Of course, cats were mummified too. Ancient Egyptians considered cats to be gods. When a cat died, their owners would shave off their own eyebrows as a sign of mourning. Nowadays, shaving eyebrows is a prank you pull on someone who is passed out drunk.

Cows are gods in India. That's where we get the expression "Holy cow!" Tom Cruise believes that he is an alien and will one day float into space. Mormons wear magic underwear. People believe lots of weird shit.

The Mind

What is "the mind" anyway? It's not the brain. They're different. This question "what is the mind?" has beguiled man for years, decades maybe. You might even say that some people have dedicated their life's work to it.

You can't touch or feel the mind. In fact, no one really knows what it looks like. I mean, unless you're on acid and then you think you know exactly what it looks like but really you're just looking at a Dorito and *thinking* that you're looking at the mind. But it's your *mind* that's thinking that. Your mind is fucked up on acid and it's making you see shit but in reality that Dorito isn't anything more than a corn chip covered in cheese powder. My advice: Eat the Dorito, drink some water, and watch TV. The effects of the acid will wear off eventually and you will realize that the entire experience was less fun in retrospect.

One thing is for certain: Your mind looks nothing like a Dorito. Prove it? I can't. Minds cannot be seen. There is no museum anywhere that I'm aware of with minds on display that you can look at. No, not even the Frick!

The mind is like tofu in that it has no particular smell. It has no particular texture or consistency. It has no temperature. It is weightless. Funny that something so central to our existence could be so elusive. Hahahahahahha. Really funny.

In a sense, the mind is *nothing* but in a sense the mind is *everything*. So which is it? Is it nothing? Or is it everything? People say the same thing about God. Either He is everything or nothing. Either you believe or you don't. Are God and the mind one and the same? To answer this question, we must delve deeper and by "deeper" I mean look it up in the dictionary because I really have no clue what it is; that's why I'm stalling so much by asking lots of rhetorical questions.

THE MIND (n.) *The mind is the human consciousness that originates in the brain and is manifested especially in thought, perception, emotion, will, memory, and imagination.*

One interesting aspect of the mind is something called *mind control.* Mind control is what happens when people use psychological tactics to subvert other people's minds. In relationship terms, this would be called *pussy whipped.* Let us ponder this term *pussy whipped.* What does it actually mean?

PUSSY WHIPPED (adj.) This is the term to describe what happens when a man is whipped by a woman's pussy. He is not in pain per se. The woman's pussy is whipping his dick and in all probability the man likes the way it feels when she whips his dick with her pussy because her pussy is awesome and he likes being whipped by it even though it's less being whipped as much as it's more like they're "having sex." It's not the typical kind of whipping because there's no actual whip involved. It's just the sensation of a man's penis inside a woman's vagina. The woman's vagina is the whip and she's whipping him but it's not shaped like a whip. It's shaped like whatever her vagina is shaped like and she's really not whipping him with it because that's not actually possible. But in a sense she is whipping him with it because she can use it to boss him around because he's afraid of it, I guess. I really don't know. I'm confused now.

Another popular form of mind control is HYPNOSIS. Hypnosis is commonly achieved by swinging one of those old-fashioned pocket watches in someone's face and saying, "You are getting very sleepy." Eventually, the subject will drift into a hypnotic state and tell you all their deepest secrets, like: "I stole my best friend's laptop and never told him. Even worse, I helped him look for it." Additionally, they will do whatever you ask them to do. Like when I was in summer camp a professional hypnotist made one my fellow campers do the funky chicken in front of everyone. It was HI-LAR-IOUS. Hypnosis is also used to help people quit smoking. However, it's a double-edged sword, because on the one hand they stop smoking but on the other hand they walk around with their arms in front of them all the time like they're sleepwalking. Or worse—they don't smoke anymore but now they can't stop doing the funky chicken.

I was introduced to my first cult in high school. It was an after-school organization called 65 Chambers. The name referred to a street in Princeton called Chambers Street and the room where we met was located at number 65. In hindsight, I see that the name had multiple meanings. These so-called 65 Chambers were the spiritual tenets of the group. These chambers (as in "dungeons") were located in our minds and there were sixty-five of them. I wonder now if they'd gotten a different room to hold their meetings, would the name have changed? 35 Chambers? Or perhaps a different street name entirely? 412 Stuckey Drive. What then? Most of the "chambers" referred to aspects of our lives that required further inspection: Do I love Jesus? Do I think Jesus is my savior? Do I think Jesus died for my sins? What are my sins? How much money do I have? Am I willing to donate this money to the group? Do I have any friends with psychological problems looking for a group of like-minded individuals? Would I be willing to talk to them about the group? Would I be willing to stress the fact that we primarily have "fun"? Would I be willing to not tell them about the Jesus stuff until they've attended their first few meetings? Would I be willing to continually pester them about it if they seemed ambivalent about it? Would I be willing to blackmail them in some way? Just stuff like that.

I grew weary of the cult after a few months. Primarily, I felt that the daily scoliosis examinations seemed unnecessary. If I don't have scoliosis on Monday, I'm probably not going have it on Tuesday either. This is to say nothing of the fact that I was quite certain that fingering my rectum and my balls should have played no part in detecting spinal irregularities.

Nowadays, cults look quite different. I call them "cliques" and they mostly involve groups of friends who feed off each other. I avoid these cults at all costs.

THE SELF-ABSORBED MIND

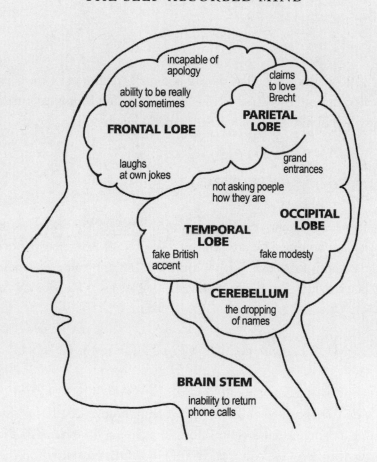

Sandwiches

I love sandwiches. I take them very seriously. In my life I have probably eaten upward of 10,000 sandwiches and that is a modest estimate. Below you will find my Golden Rules of sandwich making.

I. "BREAD IS KING"

The first rule of sandwich: Bread is king. Without bread we who make sandwich are nothing. We are nowhere. We are up shit's creek without a paddle. Bread is to sandwich what song is to band. Bread is to sandwich what shoe is to foot. Bread is to sandwich what love is to life: Bread is king.

2. "MUSTARD GOES WITH EVERYTHING"

If you have two pieces of bread, mustard, and ANYTHING ELSE, you have a delicious sandwich. Example: Bread, chicken cutlet, mustard: you have a delicious sandwich. But let's make it a little more challenging: bread, *corn on the cob*, yes, ON THE COB, mustard. You have a delicious sandwich. Bread, *box of pencils*, mustard: you have a delicious sandwich. Bread, one kind of mustard, *another kind of mustard*: you have a delicious sandwich. Mustard goes with everything and if anyone tells you that the same thing is true of mayonnaise? You tell that person that they are a liar! A fink! And a fucking asshole! Mustard goes with everything.

3. "NOTHING'S OFF-LIMITS/EVERYTHING IS IN PLAY"

Nothing's off-limits. Everything is in play. When making a sandwich you have to be willing to improvise. We don't have the luxury of a well-stocked pantry. We have to make do with what we hath. Let me ask you a question: Does grapefruit go with bologna? Yes! Nothing's off-limits. Everything is in play. Does turkey taste good covered in peanut butter? Yes. Nothing's off-limits. Everything is in play. I'm making a sandwich here! If you want a five-star meal, then go to a five-star restaurant but I'm hungry. It's two in the morning, I'm too lazy to go down to the corner deli, I have a box of yellow raisins, two mismatched pieces of bread, half a grapefruit, a slice of bologna, a bag of Twizzles, a piece of ham, four sticks of gum, a number two pencil, a jar of mustard, and I'm making a fucking sandwich. Nothing's off-limits. Everything is in play.

4. "TOAST IT"

Toast it. Toast the thing. Put the thing in a toaster and toast it. Toast the motherfucking thing.

5. "PICKLE"

Pickle. What's up, pickle? Pickle. Pickle. Pickle.

6. "SUNDRIED TOMATOES ARE TOTAL BULLSHIT"

When I said that "Nothing is off-limits and everything is in play," I was not referring to sundried tomatoes. Sundried tomatoes are the enemy of a sandwich. When you put a sundried tomato on your sandwich, it's not a sandwich anymore: it's a piece of shit. If you want to eat shit, then be my guest, but I'm hungry. It's four in the morning, I'm watching a murder doc on truTV, I need something to eat, and I don't want to eat shit. I want to eat a sandwich. Sundried tomatoes are total bullshit.

7. "THE MISSING LINK"

Okay. You've made your sandwich, you've taken a bite, but something's missing. It's not perfect. Something's wrong. What? What's wrong? What's the MISSING LINK? It's there but you need to find it. Be critical. Ask questions of your sandwich. Settle for nothing less than perfect because PERFECT is within your grasp, you fucking asshole! What's wrong with this sandwich? Does it need more mustard? Start there. Your sandwich is your life! Don't sell it short. Don't throw it away. Don't fucking one slice of cheese, one slice of bologna, wham bam thank you ma'am, fuck it, suck it. NO! This is your life we're talking about. You only live once. Find the missing link.

8. "DENIAL AIN'T JUST A RIVER IN EGYPT"

What's holding you back from your sandwich? What's keeping you from creating something that will last FOREVER!? This sandwich will last for an eternity! What are you hiding from? Secrets will kill us. Put it all out there. Expose yourself. Make yourself vulnerable. Don't be afraid of being hurt. Pain is the touchstone of growth. You can do it! You crapped in your pants once? It's okay! So have I! All the time. Your secrets are keeping you from creating a sandwich that will change people's lives! Denial Ain't Just a River in Egypt.

9. "HAVE FUN"

Have fun. Have fun making your sandwich. If it isn't fun then make something else. If you're not having fun making your fucking sandwich then make something else because making sandwiches is fucking fun!

10. "THE END"

The end is your friend. Do not fear the end. The end is life.

My Morning Routine, #5

There are certain times when no matter how hard you try—you can't sound cool. For example, I was in a drugstore the other day and I was standing in line behind a hipster girl. When she got to the counter, she asked the employee if they carried "Pepto-Bismo." *Bismo?* She purposely mispronounced it to make it seem as if she wasn't familiar with the product. Nope. You've got diarrhea, cool girl, and you can't pretend otherwise. Soooooorrrrryyyyy!!!!

I was in Milwaukee recently doing a show. The following day I was waiting in the hotel lobby to get the van back to the airport. A young twenty-something couple entered the hotel and asked the concierge if he could recommend to them a good place to eat lunch. He recommended a nearby diner. The girl seemed to have heard of the diner he recommended, got very excited, and said to her boyfriend, "This place is amazing! They've got *chicken-flavored noodles!*" The boyfriend seemed just as excited as she was. He went, "No way!? Chicken-flavored noodles?!" And then they sprinted hand in hand in the direction of the diner with the chicken-flavored noodles.

I hate it when people say to me, "Being a father is amazing—you should try it!" They say it as if it's something that I can stop doing if I don't like it, like acupuncture or Jell-O shots.

I don't understand why it is accepted practice to bum cigarettes from complete strangers. People will come up to me and be like, "Can I bum a cigarette? I'm really jonesing." But you wouldn't do that with anything else no matter how badly you wanted something. Like you wouldn't go up to someone and be like, "I'm really thirsty! Can I have a sip of your Coke?" or "Hey, I'm really horny, can I fuck your boyfriend?"

Swine Flu is such a horrible name. It's terrifying. As if *flu* wasn't bad enough on its own, they gotta add *swine* to it? Then again, anything with *flu* in the name is scary. It doesn't matter how cute the word before it is. If anything, the cuter the word before the word *flu*, the more terrifying it sounds: *Bran Muffin Flu, Marshmallow Flu, Baby Carrot Flu.*

What My Thoughts Would Look Like If You Could See Them

Part One

Other people other people other people Other people other people
Other people's lives Other people what are their lives like in comparison to my mine other people Other people are they happier than me
other people Other people other people Do they make more money
than I do Other people other people Other people should I be doing
what they're doing other people Other people they freak me out Other
people Other people Other People Other People other people Other
people other people Other people Why do they like dim sum so much
Other people other people Other people other people Other people
other people Other people Other people Other People Other People
other people people people Other people other people Other people
other people Other people other people Other people other people
Other people other people Other people other people Other people
other people Other people Other people Other People Other People
other people people people Other people other people Other people
other people Other people other people Other people other people
Other people other people Other people other people Other people
other people Other people Other people Other People Other People
other people people people Other people other people Other people
other people Other people other people Other people other people
Other people other people Other people other people Other people
other people Other people Other people Other People Other People.

What My Thoughts Would Look Like If You Could See Them

Part Two

My future. What does it look like? My future what does it look like?
My future. What does it look like? My future what does it look like?
My future. What does it look like? My future what does it look like?
My future. What does it look like? My future what does it look like?
My future. What does it look like? My future what does it look like?
My future. What does it look like? My future what does it look like?
My future. What does it look like? My future what does it look like?
My future. What does it look like? My future what does it look like?
My future. What does it look like? My future what does it look like?
My future. What does it look like? My future what does it look like?
My future. What does it look like? My future what does it look like?
My future. What does it look like? My future what does it look like?
My future. What does it look like? My future what does it look like?
My future. What does it look like? My future what does it look like?
My future. What does it look like? My future what does it look like?
My future. What does it look like? My future what does it look like?
My future. What does it look like? My future what does it look like?
My future. What does it look like? My future what does it look like?
My future. What does it look like? My future what does it look like?
My future. What does it look like? My future what does it look like?
My future. What does it look like? My future what does it look like?

Games, Puzzles, Brainteasers, Brain Twisters

I want my book to be life-altering and profound but I also want it to be fun and interactive. That's why I'm including this section called "Games, Puzzles, Brainteasers, and Brain Twisters." This way, if you're bored or just want a break from having your life altered, then you can read this section and simply just have a little fun!

Great! Let's start with a classic Brain Twister that we call "What Happened to the Dollar?"

The Scenario: Three men who do not know each other walk into a hotel and each ask for a room. The concierge informs them that there is only one room, but it has three beds in it. The men agree to take the room even though they don't know each other. The concierge tells the men that the room costs thirty dollars a night. Each of the men gives the concierge a ten dollar bill and goes up to the room. The concierge then realizes that the room only costs twenty-five dollars a night. He counts out five singles and decides that it is too complicated to divide five dollars three ways, so he gives the men back each one dollar and keeps two dollars for himself.

The Conundrum: If he gave each man back one dollar, then that means that each man spent nine dollars. Nine times three is twenty-seven, now if you add the two dollars that the concierge kept for himself then that equals twenty-nine.

The Question: What happened to the extra dollar?

The Answer: Doesn't matter. It was a nice hotel and the men turned out becoming close friends.

Here's another fun game I call "One-Minute Mysteries." This is a great game to play on a road trip with your pals. A minimum of two players are required to play. The rules of the game are simple. One player who is called the Mysterian presents the other player, who is called the Solverian, with a "mysterious circumstance." The Solverian, using questions, must then solve the mystery.

THE MYSTERIOUS CASE OF THE WOOD SHAVINGS

The Scenario: A man is found dead in a room. There is a pile of wood shavings. What happened?

Now, using questions, the Solverian must now go about the business of solving this "mysterious circumstance."

Here is a sample script:

SOLVERIAN: Is the "dead man" a midget or a dwarf?
MYSTERIAN: Yes.
SOLVERIAN: Is he a midget?
MYSTERIAN: Yes.
SOLVERIAN: Is the man a circus player?
MYSTERIAN: Yes.
SOLVERIAN: Is the man a "Shortest Man in the World" in the circus sideshow?
MYSTERIAN: Yes.
SOLVERIAN: Does he have a rival?

MYSTERIAN: Yes.

SOLVERIAN: Did the rival kill him?

MYSTERIAN: No. Not exactly.

SOLVERIAN: Did the rival precipitate his untimely death?

MYSTERIAN: Yes.

SOLVERIAN: Did the "short man" commit suicide?

MYSTERIAN: Yes.

SOLVERIAN: Did the "short man" commit suicide because he feared that he was growing taller?

MYSTERIAN: Yes.

SOLVERIAN: He feared that he was growing taller, which would mean that he was no longer the "Shortest Man in the World."

MYSTERIAN: Correct.

SOLVERIAN: His rival sanded down his cane, which made the short man think that he was growing?

MYSTERIAN: Right. Wow. You're good at this.

SOLVERIAN: Oh! Are the wood shavings in the same room as the dead man?

MYSTERIAN: No.

SOLVERIAN: Okay, so, the rival short man got ahold of the original short man's cane and sanded it down slowly over time to make the original short man think that he was growing. The wood shavings are probably in a barn somewhere. When the original short man came to the determination that he was growing, he got depressed and killed himself because he was bummed that he was no longer the shortest man in the world.

MYSTERIAN: Bingo. Nice job.

Note: The Solverian in this example got right to the heart of the matter in his first question, "Was the dead man a midget or a dwarf?" That was an excellent question and it seemed to break things wide open. Normally, it would take much longer to solve the mystery.

Here's another example, feel free to play along this time:

THE MYSTERIOUS CASE OF THE
ALBATROSS SANDWICH

MYSTERIAN: Two men walk into a roadside diner. One of the men orders the albatross sandwich and says to the other man, "For good old time's sake." He takes one bite of the sandwich, swallows, and then runs outside onto the highway and throws himself in front of an oncoming bus and dies. What happened?

SOLVERIAN #2: You just explained what happened.

MYSTERIAN: Right, but why did he do that?

SOLVERIAN #2: Why does anyone do anything? Life is chaotic in that way.

MYSTERIAN: You're not playing the game!

SOLVERIAN #2: Okay. He was depressed and suicidal about something unrelated? His wife was cheating on him or something.

MYSTERIAN: Nope.

SOLVERIAN #2: I don't fucking know. This game is stupid.

[In this sample text, the Solverian is much less clever than the Solverian in the first sample. Let's bring in our original Solverian to help him solve the mystery.]

ORIGINAL SOLVERIAN: Were the men both in the Navy together many years ago?

MYSTERIAN: Yes.

ORIGINAL SOLVERIAN: Were they shipwrecked at some point?

MYSTERIAN: Yes.

ORIGINAL SOLVERIAN: Were they eating the dead sailors to stay alive?

MYSTERIAN: Yes, but...

ORIGINAL SOLVERIAN: Whoever was in charge was telling everybody that they were eating albatross?

MYSTERIAN: Precisely.

ORIGINAL SOLVERIAN: So, many years later, these two men, both sailors on that boat, went to a diner and one of them ordered albatross "for old time's sake." When he tasted it, he realized that it tasted nothing like the albatross he'd been eating on the shipwrecked boat. He put two and two together. He realized they were eating each other. He got bummed out about it and killed himself.

MYSTERIAN: Right.

SOLVERIAN #2: That's bullshit. What's albatross?

MYSTERIAN: It's an aquatic seabird, you fucking dick.

ORIGINAL SOLVERIAN: Well, by definition, if it's a seabird it's also aquatic.

MYSTERIAN: You shut up too, dickhead. I'm tired from all this driving. Let's take a pit stop. I need to stretch.

THE MYSTERIOUS CASE OF THE
ONE-WAY TICKET

MYSTERIAN: A man and a woman go on a second honeymoon to the Swiss Alps. While hiking in the Alps, the man pushes his wife over the edge of an alp and she falls to her death. No one saw it happen. There were no eyewitnesses. When he returned to the bottom of the alp, he reported to the local authorities that she had fallen to her untimely death. He was allowed to return to America on his own recognizance. Months passed. He believed that he had committed a perfect murder. One day he got a knock on his door...

SOLVERIAN #2: Come on, already! Is this like the longest fucking setup or what?!

MYSTERIAN: Asshole! Syracuse is like another 200 miles away! What are we going to talk about? Who gives a shit if it's long? You're not going to figure it out anyway!

SOLVERIAN #2: Fine.

MYSTERIAN: Anyway, he gets a knock on his door and it's the local authorities. They charge him with murder. How did they know he was guilty?

SOLVERIAN #2: Someone saw him push her?

MYSTERIAN: What did I fucking say? What did I fucking say?

SOLVERIAN #2: About what?! And slow the fuck down! You're doing like 90 miles per hour…

MYSTERIAN: I said that no one saw him push her. There were no eyewitnesses.

SOLVERIAN #2: Maybe there was one, though.

MYSTERIAN: There wasn't! Jesus, what's your problem?

SOLVERIAN #2: What's *your* problem? You've been acting like a huge dick ever since last night!

MYSTERIAN: Yeah, because you cockblocked me last night at that bar!

SOLVERIAN #2: She wasn't into you at all, dude. You're just pissed because I macked with her in the potty.

MYSTERIAN: She was into me and then you swooped in and stole her. Besides which, who says "macked"? Who says that?

SOLVERIAN #2: She wasn't into you, okay?

MYSTERIAN: She was into me, okay? I could tell.

SOLVERIAN #2: Yeah? How?

MYSTERIAN: Forget it. Let's just drive in silence for a bit.

SOLVERIAN #2: Look, Matt, I'm sorry if you're pissed at me. I really don't know what to say. I can't really help it if you're upset but I honestly have to say that I don't think I did anything wrong.

MYSTERIAN: Let's just forget about it.

SOLVERIAN #2: Sure, whatever.

Time passes.

SOLVERIAN #2: I don't know how they knew. Maybe they had a hunch. I really don't know.

[At this point, Solverian #1 is woken up from his nap and is asked to solve the mystery.]

SOLVERIAN #1: Did he buy himself a round-trip ticket to the
    Swiss Alps?
MYSTERIAN: Yes.
SOLVERIAN #1: Did he buy her a one-way ticket?
MYSTERIAN: Yep.
SOLVERIAN #1: So that's how they knew.
MYSTERIAN: Exactly.

20 QUESTIONS AND ITS VARIABLES

A really fun two-player game is 20 Questions. The rules are simple:
Player A thinks of "a mineral," "a vegetable," or "an animal." Player B
has twenty yes or no questions to ask in an attempt to figure out what
"mineral, vegetable, or animal" Player A is thinking of. The strategy is
for Player B to use his questions wisely in an effort to whittle down the
possibilities and ultimately arrive at the correct answer.

Here's a sample script. (Hint: Player A is thinking of a dog.)

PLAYER A: I'm thinking of a mineral, a vegetable, or an animal.
    You have twenty questions to figure out what I'm thinking of.
PLAYER B: Is it a dog?
PLAYER A: Yes!

Okay. So that was pretty easy. Usually it's a bit trickier than that. Here's
another example where Player B needs to probe a little deeper before
arriving at an answer.

PLAYER A: I'm thinking of a mineral, a vegetable, or an animal.
    You have twenty questions to figure out what I'm thinking of.
PLAYER B: Are you thinking of a vegetable?
PLAYER A: Yes.
PLAYER B: Is it a carrot?
PLAYER A: Yes.

Still pretty easy, right? But here's a trickier example. In this example, Player A will make it a little harder for Player B by requiring him to be a bit more specific with his answer.

PLAYER A: I'm thinking of a mineral, a vegetable, or an animal. You have twenty questions to figure out what I'm thinking of.

PLAYER B: Are you thinking of a vegetable?

PLAYER A: Yes.

PLAYER B: Is it a carrot?

PLAYER A: No.

PLAYER B: Is it *the* carrot?

PLAYER A: Yes.

See? That was trickier. Player A wasn't thinking of just any old carrot. He was thinking of a very specific carrot. It's sneaky but totally legal and well within the rules. Let's look at yet another, even trickier, example.

PLAYER A: I'm thinking of a mineral, a vegetable, or an animal. You have twenty questions to figure out what I'm thinking of.

PLAYER B: Are you thinking of a vegetable?

PLAYER A: Yes.

PLAYER B: Is it a carrot?

PLAYER A: No.

PLAYER B: Is it *the* carrot?

PLAYER A: No.

PLAYER B: Is it just "carrot"?

PLAYER A: Yes.

In this game, Player A was thinking of not just any old carrot, nor was he thinking of any one carrot in particular, he was thinking of "carrot" in the larger sense of "carrot." Again, it's totally legal and within the boundaries of the rules.

We've been using pretty common things like "dog" and "carrot" but most of the time, Player A will think of something a little more obscure than a carrot. Let's look at another sample script. This time Player A is thinking of something a little more obscure than just a "dog" or a "carrot." (Hint: Player A is thinking of an "Alaskan Snow Frog.")

> PLAYER A: I'm thinking of a mineral, a vegetable, or an animal. You have twenty questions to figure out what I'm thinking of.
> PLAYER B: Are you thinking of a vegetable?
> PLAYER A: No.
> PLAYER B: Are you thinking of a mineral?
> PLAYER A: No.
> PLAYER B: Are you thinking of an animal?
> PLAYER A: Yes.

Okay, let's look at this. Player B just made a potentially fatal error. He didn't need to ask if it was an animal! Since he already knew it wasn't a vegetable or a mineral, he should have known that the only other possibility was "animal" and that he didn't need to ask. What a dick!

> PLAYER B: Is it a frog?
> PLAYER A: No.
> PLAYER B: Is it *the* frog?
> PLAYER A: No. That's five questions by the way.
> PLAYER B: Is it just "frog"?
> PLAYER A: No.
> PLAYER B: Is it a specific type of frog?
> PLAYER A: Yes.
> PLAYER B: Is it a frog species specific to the North American continent?
> PLAYER A: Yes.
> PLAYER B: Is it a frog species that lives in a cold weather climate?
> PLAYER A: Yes.
> PLAYER B: Is it a cold climate frog species that lives in the United States?

PLAYER A: Yes.

PLAYER B: Is it a cold climate frog species that lives in the contiguous United States?

PLAYER A: No.

PLAYER B: Interesting. So is it Hawaii?

Player B just made another potentially fatal error! He didn't need to ask if it was from Hawaii because he already knew that the frog was a cold climate species.

PLAYER A: No.

PLAYER B: So is it Alaska?

PLAYER A: Yes. That's thirteen questions.

Player B just made another potentially fatal error! He didn't need to ask if it was from Alaska! Since he already knew it wasn't from Hawaii! The only noncontiguous state left is Alaska. Player B just burned two questions for nothing. What a dick!

PLAYER B: Is it the Alaskan Mountain Frog?

PLAYER A: No.

PLAYER B: Is it the Alaskan River Frog?

PLAYER A: No. That's fifteen questions.

PLAYER B: Is it a snow frog?

PLAYER A: No.

PLAYER B: Is it *the* snow frog?

PLAYER A: No.

PLAYER B: Is it a type of snow frog?

PLAYER A: Yes.

PLAYER B: Is it the Alaskan Snow Frog?

PLAYER A: No. That's nineteen questions.

PLAYER B: Is it just "Alaskan Snow Frog"?

PLAYER A: No. Sorry. That was twenty questions.

PLAYER B: What was the answer?

PLAYER A: The answer was "an Alaskan Snow Frog."
PLAYER B: Dammit! I was gonna guess that!

Player B has only himself to blame for this defeat. He burned three questions out of sheer stupidity.

Now, 20 Questions is fun but some people find it too easy. For those advanced players there's 200 Questions. In 200 Questions the rules are exactly the same. Whereas 20 Questions is a good game to play on a short drive, 200 Questions can take many hours and is good to play on a long drive, or if you're stuck somewhere.

Here's a sample script of 200 Questions. (Hint: Player A is thinking of a dog.)

PLAYER A: I'm thinking of a mineral, a vegetable, or an animal. You have two hundred questions to figure out what I'm thinking of.
PLAYER B: Is it an animal?
PLAYER A: Yes.
PLAYER B: Is it a dog?
PLAYER A: Yes.

Now, the interesting thing about 200 Questions is that sometimes it doesn't take any longer to play than it does to play 20 Questions. It really all depends on the intelligence of the person asking the questions.

But let's say you've really got a lot of time on your hands and 200 Questions isn't meaty enough for you. Like, let's say that you and another person are stranded on a desert island with no chance of rescue. If that's your situation, then I suggest you play 1,000 Questions. The rules are exactly the same but the games can last much longer. It's a great way to pass the time. If it's the right game, it could last days!

Let's look at a sample script of 1,000 Questions. (Hint: Player A is thinking of a carrot.)

PLAYER A: I'm thinking of a mineral, a vegetable, or an animal.
  You have one thousand questions to figure out what I'm
  thinking of.
PLAYER B: Is it an animal?
PLAYER A: No.
PLAYER B: Is it a mineral?
PLAYER A: No.
PLAYER B: So then is it a vegetable?
PLAYER A: Yes.

Okay, let's look at this. Player B just made a potentially fatal error. He didn't need to ask if it was a vegetable! Since he already knew it wasn't an animal or a mineral, he should have known that the only other possibility was "vegetable" and that he didn't need to ask. What a dick! However, because this is 1,000 Questions and not 20 Questions, there is a greater margin for error, so Player B's fuckup may not hurt him that badly in the long run.

PLAYER B: Is it a carrot?
PLAYER A: Yes.

Okay, so in this example Player B was able to make up for his error in question 3 and bounce back strong in question 4 and get the right answer with 996 questions still left to ask. Good save, Player B!

Now the last variation of 20 Questions is Bajillion Questions and it's best for players who have unlimited time resources. Typically these are (a) immortals, (b) vampires, or (c) Gods.

Here's a sample game of Bajillion Questions. (Hint: Player A is thinking of a carrot.)

PLAYER A: I'm thinking of a mineral, a vegetable, or an animal. You have a bajillion questions to figure out what I'm thinking of.

PLAYER B: Is it an animal?

PLAYER A: No.

PLAYER B: I hate being immortal. Everyone I've ever loved has died. It's impossible to get close to anyone because eventually they will grow old and die but I will live on and carry the burden of history on my shoulders.

PLAYER A: I'm a God. I have compassion for you and I can sympathize but I can't honestly say that I *empathize*. I exist in a permanent state of pure enlightenment. It's awesome.

PLAYER B: Yeah. I hear you.

PLAYER A: You want to finish the game?

PLAYER B: Not really.

PLAYER A: Okay.

Drinking Games!

Parties are all about fun and there's nothing more fun than a really good drinking game. Drinking games are fun because they bring people together, they are very entertaining, but most importantly, they get you really drunk really fast. We've all heard of Beer Pong and Thumper and Quarters, but here are five suggestions for some of my favorite drinking games that you may not have heard of.

You Chug: In the game of You Chug, all that is required is two or more players and lots of beer. The rules are simple: The players assemble together in a room. Each player should have a large container of beer. One player volunteers to start chugging. After he has chugged as much beer as he can, he then points to another player and exclaims, "You chug!" At that point, the player who has been pointed to lifts his beer to his mouth and begins to chug. When he is done chugging he then points to another player — it could be the first player if he wants — and says, "You chug." This pretty much continues until everyone doesn't want to play anymore.

You Drink: The game of You Drink is very similar to the game of You Chug with one significant variation. In the game of You Drink, the players will say "You drink" instead of "You chug." Other than that, it's the same.

Beer Scrabble: Some people like a drinking game that is a little more strategy-oriented than You Chug and its close relative You Drink. For those of you who fit into that category, may I suggest Beer Scrabble? The rules of Beer Scrabble are very simple: You play Scrabble and drink beer while you play. (Variations of Beer Scrabble include Wine Scrabble, Rum Scrabble, and Vodka Scrabble. If these variations aren't enough for you, may I suggest thinking of your own variations based on what kind of alcohol you want to drink and then just add the word *Scrabble* to it?)

Beer Sudoku: Sometimes you're in the mood to play a drinking game but you have no one to play with. This is probably a sign that you have a serious drinking problem but it's not my place to judge. For those of you who want to know of a great drinking game that you can play alone, may I suggest Beer Sudoku? Beer Sudoku is as much fun as regular Sudoku but with beer. Now if you don't like playing Sudoku but still want to play a drinking game alone, I can suggest Beer Crossword Puzzle, Beer Read a Book, or Beer Drink Alone.

Find the Sandwich: In this game, the drinking will have happened the night before. The object of the game is to find the sandwich that you started eating in your apartment the night before, right before you passed out on the sofa. When you find the sandwich, or what's left of it, you throw it away and give yourself a "point."

"YOU CHUG"

Player C begins the game by drinking as much beer as he/she possibly can.

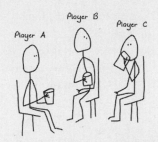

Player C finishes chugging. Player C points to Player A and exclaims, "You chug!" (Some players will prefer to say "Now *you* chug!" This is an acceptable variation.)

Player A now chugs. Player C demonstrates that you're allowed to chug even when it's not your turn.

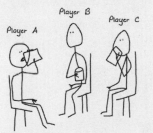

Now player A points to Player B and says, "Now you chug!" and so on... (Nota bene: Player A does have the option of pointing finger back at Player C if he/she so desires.)

At a certain point the players will be shitfaced. This is indicated by their slumped postures and the "x" marks they have for eyes. (*Note also that Player B holds a cellphone and has presumably been drunk dialing his ex-girlfriend.)

The game has unquestionably devolved at this point. Player C has chosen not to say "You chug!" and instead is improvising his own dialogue. Player B has gotten through to his ex-girlfriend and seems to have left the game. Player A is gettin kinda sad.

Game is now over because Player B left; Player C is passed out; and Player A is dry-heaving.

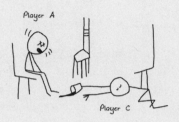

Scrabble

I'm obsessed with Scrabble and I'm really good at it. Just to show you what I mean, I saved a recent game that I played against a very formidable opponent and kept copious notes on.

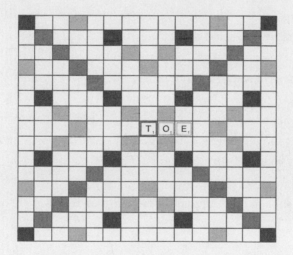

This was my formidable opponent's first maneuver. He formulated the word *toe*. This was a really good play if you're a four-year-old boy or a common buffoon. In utilizing the mandatory double word score on the first move, his maneuver garnered him a small but tidy sum of six points.

Now, being the expert, I am always looking to maximize my point values. Scanning my tile board, I saw the letters *F, D, O, L, O, C, G*. My first move is the word *flood*.

With *flood*, I make not one but three separate words in one fell swoop. (Now, it must be said that I don't know what a "fell swoop" is but I know for a fact that in context it makes perfect sense. I learned this descriptive couplet from my father, who has a very antique vocabulary.) I made the words *of, flood,* and *el. El* spells the letter *L.*

Ell also spells the letter *L.* Knowing good two-letter words is key to attaining Scrabble prowess. Other good two-letter words are: *aa, oe, ai, fe,* and *baa.* Now, technically, *baa* isn't a two-letter word. However, it is the sound that a sheep makes.

Here is a look at the scorecard after two moves:

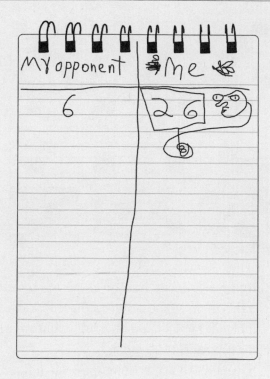

It is probably worth noting that in this particular instant I was the player keeping score.

My opponent for his second move chooses to form the word *hat*. He seemed not to pick up on the strategy of creating more than one word with each separate turn, thus accumulating additional points. Scrabble is a game of points. Choice of word and length of word, though aesthetically pleasing, is ultimately trumped by points. Points are everything in Scrabble.

Nothing against my opponent, but this move is a travesty. All he got was six points. By this point in the contest, I have lost all respect for my adversary. I smell blood. I am a large buzzard circling a rotting carcass below me. (Haha. I just said "blow me.")

I know that my next move needs to be spectacular. I am always looking for an opportunity to play what is known as a "bingo." A bingo occurs when the Scrabble player uses all seven of his tiles in one turn. As a reward for this special achievement, the player receives an additional fifty points over and above whatever board value the word earned. My next move:

Felchings is the plural of *felching*. So, used in a sentence, I might say, "I went to a big party last night at a friend of a friend's house. The party was fun but unusual. There were multiple felchings happening when I walked in the door." If you don't know what the word *felching* means, I suggest you google it.

This is my opponent's next move:

It's a good move because he's utilizing the available triple word score for the word *socks*. This move earns him respectable point values and in using the *K* and *C* he is maximizing his point accumulation.

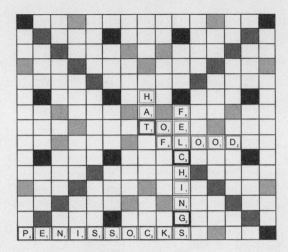

Here I make the word the *penissocks*. I do this by utilizing the available triple word score box to the left of *socks*.

Before pulling new tiles, I look down at my unused tiles and I see that I have an *E* and an *R*. I realize that I can make the word *penissockser*, which gives me another bingo.

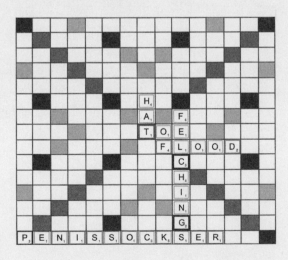

This move prompts my opponent to "challenge." By challenging an opponent's word, you are taking a calculated risk. If their word is valid, then the challenger loses his turn. If the word is invalid, then it is the challengee whose turn is lost. So we break out the *OED* and look it up. Sure enough it's in there.

> *penissockser* n. (pee-niss-sox-ur) 1. a penissock maker. 2. a wearer of penissocks. 3. also, "penis soccer": playing soccer with your penis (see also: *pussy soccer*).

At this point, it's fair to say that I'm blowing this guy out. He loses his turn for the bad challenge, which of course means that I get to go again. I'm eyeballing *hat* in the middle of the board and decide to make *shat* and *shat* in the same turn.

I look at my remaining tiles—*E*, *R*, and *P*—and I see that I can play another bingo and add *pre* to *shat*, thus forming the word *preshat* and creating for myself an additional fifty points.

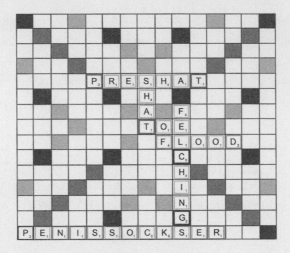

To my utter shock and dismay, my opponent sees fit to challenge yet again. This time the word in question is *preshat*. Once again, the *OED* is broken out.

> **preshat** adv. (pree-shat) 1. the stuff that happened right before someone took a shit. *Used in a sentence*: "Bob shat. Preshat, he responded to a backlog of email, chomped on his lady's cooter, and finished that jigsaw puzzle he'd been working on for months of the kitten caught up in a ball of yarn."

He loses another turn. I see another opportunity to utilize the triple word score and make...

Reunshat, which inexplicably he challenges. Leaving me no option but to go back to the *OED* for a third time.

reunshat v. (ree-on-shaat) 1. the act of having decided yet again not to shit that other time before when you also didn't shit.

It's a whitewash. This is the scorecard after *penissockser*.

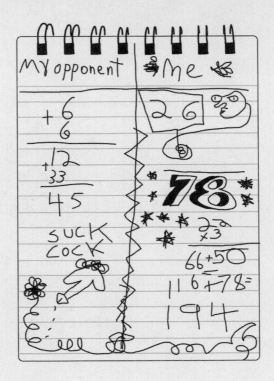

Upstairs/Downstairs

As I stated earlier, in my perfect world order, loud music will be banned. I will extend that further to say that all loud noises will be banned. With these exceptions:

1. Thunderclaps
2. Bruce Springsteen concerts
3. Anything elephant-related

If it's not one of the above loud noises, then it will be banned in my perfect world order.

Loud construction noises will be first on my agenda. Lately, I have construction going on outside my apartment; this morning started with the foreman telling his workers, "Okay, guys! Start making as much noise as possible until the one o'clock lunch break. Then resume your loud noises until five, and we'll pick up where we left off tomorrow morning."

Second on my agenda will be sirens. This includes sirens from ambulances, police cars, and fire trucks. I realize that these people are saving lives, but don't they realize that I'm trying to think?

Third on my agenda will be loud music. I save the worst for last. This pertains specifically to my former downstairs neighbors, who seemed to believe that our apartment building was a college frat house.

There had to be at least seven of them living down there, and they all had "nouveau-dude" names like Oscar, Nils, and Lars. Three of them were named Josh. I could barely tell them apart. They all wore the same clothes: hooded sweatshirts, green army pants, and knit caps.

As best I could tell, all seven of them were aspiring "world music" DJs. They blasted Gypsy Kings remixes at all hours of the day and night. The vibrations from their bass amp made my walls pulsate.

My angry visits to their front door imploring them to "please turn down the bass" had become a nightly ritual. Clad only in boxers and a T-shirt, I would knock loudly eight or nine times before they answered the door because the music drowned out the sound of my pounding fist. Once they finally answered, I'd be greeted threateningly by at least three of them at once as a huge cartoon cloud of pot smoke billowed out of their apartment and into the stairwell.

They detested me. They simply couldn't understand how some- one their age could object to their nonstop partying. Our interactions became increasingly confrontational, and on several occasions I even armed myself with a tennis racquet in case things got out of hand.

The last thing I ever wanted was to become "that guy." Yet I had become my own worst nightmare—Mr. Roper from the sitcom *Three's Company.* I had become the jerkoff upstairs neighbor pounding on the floor with a broomstick, raining on everyone's parade.

Still, it seemed like a huge injustice to me. I was paying rent, wasn't I? Why should my life be made into a living hell? If peace and quiet came at the price of being Mr. Roper, then I was willing to make that trade-off.

One day, I stopped one of the aspiring world music DJs in the hallway as he lugged his ten-speed bike up the stairwell on his shoulder. I tried to bargain with him. I said, "Listen, Josh. Just let me know about your all-night keg parties in advance. That way I can make alternate plans to be out of the country, and I then I won't complain." Josh seemed cool with that. An agreement had been reached. He took off his fingerless gloves, extended his hand, and we shook. The very next day there was a letter under my door.

Hey Michael,
    It's Oscar, Lars, Nils, Judah, Josh, Josh, and Josh from
downstairs. This Friday night we're having a small get-together.

It shouldn't be that big, no more than sixty people. We're getting
two kegs and a ten-feet-long hoagie and Josh is going to spin world
music. Please feel free to stop by.
  Best Wishes,
  The Guys from #1A

The letter impressed me. This really seemed like progress. I gladly
made alternate plans for that Friday night—I bought a big book about
the history of influenza and reserved a room at a nearby Holiday Inn
Express. That evening I learned all about how thousands of people had
died of the flu and I got a great night's sleep.

When I arrived back at my apartment the following morning, the
hallways inside the building were fully coated in a thin glaze of party
slime. The stairwell reeked of alcohol, hoagie, and sweat. There were
cigarette butts, empty beer cans, and wine bottles everywhere. I was
euphoric that I had been absent for the creation of this mess.

Later that night, while preparing a home-cooked meal, I noticed the
sounds of laughter and dance remixes coming from downstairs. They
were having another party, but this time there was no letter of warning.
I became enraged and immobilized by anger. My anger mushroomed
into a full-blown panic attack. I fumed. I seethed. I passed out. The
next morning, I fired off a letter. It read:

Dear Downstairs Neighbors,
  First of all, thank you for your letter this week. I really
appreciated you taking the time to give me forewarning of your
party Friday night, and judging by how badly the hallway reeked
of pot and beer, I'd say the party must have been a great
success.
  I'm sorry I couldn't make it, but I already went to college fifteen
years ago, and while I didn't particularly enjoy crowded beer
parties then, I certainly don't enjoy them now, what with me being
in my mid-thirties and all. But, given that you're also in your mid-
thirties, I guess you don't need me to tell you that.

That said, I was a little bit surprised when, the very next night, last night, you had another loud party and didn't write me about it. It's not that I don't like hearing your Ziggy Marley live bootleg mix tapes blasting at full volume through the floorboards, it's just that I had planned to have a quiet night in, and your little gathering/gypsy revival somewhat ruined it for me.

Still, I didn't want to be a dick and ask you to turn down the music, so I wrapped a J.Crew sweater around my head, curled up into the fetal position, and hid under my covers. The good news is that I was able to go to sleep. The bad news is that it didn't happen until five-thirty in the morning, when your drum circle ended.

In the spirit of being a good neighbor, I'm writing you this letter to give you fair warning that next weekend I am having a "quiet night in." The "quiet night in" will start at five o'clock on Friday afternoon and will continue all the way into the following morning. For my "quiet night in," please be warned I will not be listening to any loud music from five o'clock until roughly eight p.m. After that, I will continue to not be listening to any loud music for the rest of the night and into the following rest of my life. I will, however, quietly go about my business, answering emails, folding laundry, and meticulously hand painting small figurines of seventeenth-century French peasants.

And, please note: The vaguely "hallway-ish" smell in the hallway will be the smell the hallway always has, because I will not be using the hallway for any reason during my quiet night in. If this in any way inconveniences you, I apologize and would be more than willing to discuss further.

Finally, I'd like to apologize for the unannounced "quiet nights in" that I've been having every night since I moved in three years ago. I realize that it is a common courtesy to inform each other of these things and given that you've shown me the respect of letting me know in advance about your drunken frat parties, I should extend the same courtesy to you. I can well understand that the

amount of noise I don't make must be extremely not disturbing to
you in any way, and for this, I apologize. Again, if you would like
to discuss further, do not hesitate to call or knock.

Best wishes,

Your upstairs neighbor, Michael[13]

Eventually, I resorted to banging on the floor with a broom. This seemed to work, but as soon as my downstairs neighbors stopped making noise, my upstairs neighbors, a newly minted couple, picked up the slack. Every night at one in the morning a "hammering" sound from above would resonate through my bedroom. Not "hammering" like two people having sex, it was more of a "blunt object hitting wood" sort of hammering. It would be intermittent and it would last for hours. It got to the point where I actually longed for the Gypsy Kings remixes.

By the sounds of it, I postulated that they were cobbling shoes. Cobbling shoes seemed like a cool "new couple activity" but not at one in the morning. One night, I couldn't take it anymore, so I ventured upstairs to complain. My upstairs neighbor opened the door for me but only a crack, just the length of the chain on the door, which he hadn't removed. It was sort of creepy, like he didn't want me to see inside. He peered out at me and said, very flatly, "What?"

"I just wanted to ask if you guys could stop cobbling shoes so loudly?" I asked innocently.

"We're not cobbling shoes," he sniped.

"Oh," I said, "I just assumed that you were."

"My girlfriend is making jewelry," he said proudly.

"That's cool," I said. "Does she have to work from one in the morning until four in the morning or is it a project she could work on during waking hours?"

"I manage a bar and so she waits for me to get home before she starts," he said. I didn't know he managed a bar. Last I heard he was an actuary.

---

13. I decided not to send it: restraint of pen and tongue (aka "being a chicken").

"Yeah, well, it's just that I have to get up early in the morning and the cobbling is very disruptive."

"I really feel like you're trying to tell me how to live my life," he said.

"Not at all," I said matter-of-factly. "I just can't sleep if you're banging on the floor all night long."

"She's not banging on the floor," he said. "She's banging on a table." He grunted and closed the door.

After this, the banging stopped, which was a good thing, but a few days later, instead of banging, they seemed to be dragging heavy objects across the floor during roughly the same hours of night. I postulated that they were either:

a) Moving furniture
b) Storing large sacks of potatoes
c) Dragging corpses into a freezer

The first night that my girlfriend Kalin slept over, she asked me what the noise upstairs was. I said, "They're just dragging dead bodies around. Don't worry. It will stop in a few hours."

Eventually the dragging of dead bodies stopped too. No world music, no hammering, and no corpse dragging. I had a solid fortnight of quiet. Then the vacuuming began. Day and night, my upstairs neighbors vacuumed their apartment. I can only assume that they had the single cleanest and most dust free carpet of all time. This is no small feat, and while I can identify with incapacitating obsessive-compulsive behavior, I really couldn't imagine how much dirtier their rug could have gotten from nine p.m. to ten p.m. because they'd vacuum usually from four or five p.m. until nine p.m. then take a break (dinner?) and then resume vacuuming until midnight.

I can't understand people who willfully disrupt their neighbors. I am the opposite. To me, it's just as much of an invasion of privacy to be heard by other people as it is to be the one doing the hearing.

I used to live in an apartment in Carroll Gardens, Brooklyn, and the woman below me complained that she could hear me "walking around." While I was sympathetic to her plight, I also felt that it was unreasonable for her to ask me to stop "walking around," what with it being my own apartment and all. What was I supposed to do? Crawl? Fly? I told her that if I could fly, I would, but I might not be able to avoid "walking around" until I was able to learn how to fly. She continued to complain. The irrationality of her complaint annoyed me, but I really didn't like knowing that she could hear me either, so I bought a pair of those gigantic slippers from Target and wore them around my house.

Good Penis vs. Bad Penis

Hotels have a very specific smell, I've noticed. It's kind of a good smell because it's familiar. It's that "this hotel smells like a hotel" smell. I think I've figured out what the smell is. It's a combination of soap, socks, and penis. But it's a good penis smell, not a bad penis smell. You know? It's good, clean, limp penis. Very clean and freshly toweled penis. Good, clean, limp, innocuous, fluffy penis. Well-meaning, sweet penis. Not sweet like candy. Sweet like, "He's so sweet." You know? Like, "Isn't that guy Bob sweet?" Good, clean, sweet, dear penis. And not like, "Dear Penis, How are you?" It's not a letter. We're not talking about writing a letter to a penis. I'm saying, dear penis. Like, "That penis is so dear and sweet." And not a deer's penis either. Just a dear, sweet, fluffy, freshly toweled penis.

Bad penis is totally different. Bad penis is like when you go to the Econo Lodge because it's cheaper and then you get to your room and you're like, "It's smells like BAD PENIS in here! This room smells like bad, intellectually curious penis! Grab your shit, we're leaving! We're going to the Holiday Inn Express up the road where it smells like good penis!" There is nothing worse or more terrifying than an intellectually curious penis.

Hotels can be bad but I hate flying the most. I hate waiting in security lines. Why do I need to take off my shoes? They built a machine that can fly but I have to take my shoes off? I mean, come on! If Orville and Wilbur Redenbacher could invent an airplane, you'd think that they'd figure out a way to let us keep our goddam shoes on! And those goddam bins! Why do I have to put everything in a bin?! They built a machine that can fly but I have to put my goddam shoes in a bin!? And why can't I bring a normal-size container of toothpaste with me?! I mean, they built a machine that can fly, you'd think it'd be okay to put a normal-size tube of toothpaste in my backpack. And let's get real—if I'm smart enough to fit a bomb inside a normal-size tube of toothpaste, chances are I'll find a way to fit it into a smaller tube of toothpaste too.

After the bins, now I'm in the "terminal" and I'm shelling out fifteen dollars for a chicken salad sandwich on pumpernickel bread, except that the sandwich doesn't taste like chicken salad or pumpernickel, it tastes like what an airport smells like: dead, lifeless, slightly farty air. You know? Like tens of thousands of people lugging bags around farting for hours in an air-compressed chamber. So essentially, I bought a fifteen dollar "fart wrap."

Then there's that weird tunnel you have to walk on that goes from the gate inside of the airplane. It's wall-to-wall carpeted and there's no air in it! And it's always backed up! I feel like I'm inside a giant worm. I call it a "fuck tunnel" because it's so fucking claustrophobic.

One time I sat next to an attractive woman on an airplane. Upon seeing her, I thought we might join "The Mile High Club."

"The Mile High Club," for those of you not in the know, is when you fuck in midair. And by "fuck in midair" I don't mean, like, you jump up into the air and fuck really fast before your feet hit the ground, no I'm saying that you have sex in the airplane. It's a very special club. As of this writing, I'm still not a member.

I had it all figured out: I'd lean over halfway into the flight and whisper in her ear, "Hey…um…I'm gonna just head into the bathroom and take a shit because I ate a fifteen-dollar chicken salad sandwich on pumpernickel which, combined with all the air pressure inside the cabin, means I'm, like, basically a balloon that's fixing to pop. So why don't you wait, like, ten or fifteen minutes and then come tippy-tap on the door and I'll let you in and we'll fuuuuuuuuccccck." I had it all figured out.

As soon as I sat down next to her, before the plane even started to move, she pulled her cell phone out of her handbag and began to energetically write a text message. I surreptitiously leaned over and read her text without her knowing. It said, "Why do I always have to sit next to the smelly, hipster guy!???!!!"

I was grief-stricken. First of all, didn't she know? I'm not a hipster! I'm a metrosexual. Secondly, I don't smell! I pride myself on that. If anything, I have no discernable scent of any kind. I'm like human tofu. Thirdly, any hopes of fucking in midair were dashed in an instant. I sat in complete paralysis for the entire flight trying to decide how to respond to this injustice. It was a bit of a conundrum because if I told her I read her text then she would know I snooped, but if I didn't say anything, then I could never look at myself in the mirror again. I said nothing the entire flight. I just sat there, frozen. I only got up once to go to the bathroom and deflate.

As we deboarded the plane and walked through the "fuck tunnel" into the terminal, I decided to make my move. I ran up to her, heart pounding, and I said: "Hey!" She stopped walking and looked at me quizzically. I made direct eye contact, tears almost welling up in my eyes. "I'm sorry you had to sit next to me on the plane!" I said.

She seemed genuinely confused and said, "What are talking about?"

Then I zinged her. I said, "I know I must *smell* pretty bad."

Then I stormed off. Oh snap!

As I walked away, I had a feeling of total and complete vindication, as though I'd just slayed (slewn?) a dragon. I felt very, *very* good about myself. That was until I started to replay the exchange in my mind. I realized that I'd essentially only confirmed what she'd said about me in her text. More than that, *I'd apologized for it*. It was not a victory for me. It was a victory for her! I spent the next half hour running, gooselike, through the airport, looking for her so that I could zing her better. But she was gone. She probably got picked up at the baggage claim by her nonhipster, cologne-drenched boyfriend.

Uncreative Nonfiction

I've realized that my memoir isn't really taking shape the way that I had hoped. I guess that in order to write a memoir you have to have a "story" to tell. I turned on my computer and decided to write something deep and meaningful, for a change.

I don't understand why men wash their hands after they pee. My penis is clean! I'm not going to get my hands dirty from touching my penis. I shower every morning. It's covered in two layers of cloth, sometimes three when I'm wearing snow pants. If anything I should be washing my hands before I pee. My penis is the one at risk of getting dirty. And if I'm not going to wash my hands before I pee, then I should be washing my penis after I pee, not my hands. They should put a loaf of sliced bread right by the sink in bathrooms, and after you've washed your penis, you just wrap a piece of bread around your penis and squeeze. That would be a very clean and comfy way of drying your penis after you wash it. I guess maybe some guys need to wash their hands after they pee because they have a whale spout penis. Guys who have whale spout penises tend to splash their pee around because their pee shoots upward when they pee. Still, for any guy reading this who has a whale spout penis, don't be ashamed because a whale spout penis can really come in handy if there's a power outage and the lights go off—yep, because if you have a whale spout penis, then you can use the blubber from your penis to make a candle.

I pressed Save. I paused. *I can't do this.* I have nothing to say of any importance. Maybe I'll invent a new book genre: Uncreative Nonfiction. I called Ben that afternoon and told him that I had changed my mind and wanted to switch directions. I told him that I wanted to write a book of "uncreative nonfiction." He asked what that would be. I said it would be just what it sounds like, uncreative and nonfiction. Like maybe a story about how stuffy my apartment gets sometimes during the winter. He said that I should write about it and show it to him. I turned the computer back on and wrote feverishly.

Last night I climbed into bed next to my girlfriend. "The snow has stopped falling. It's 30 degrees outside," I told her.

"So?" she asked. She was groggy from a full day's work and already drifting off to sleep.

"Don't you get it?" I said. "That means the heater is going to turn on. When it's cold outside the heater turns on automatically."

"Good," she said softly.

"No. You don't understand!" I exclaimed.

"What's wrong?" she asked and sat up in the bed and put her arm around me in an effort to console me. "You seem upset."

"It's going to get really stuffy in here," I said.

"Can't you turn it off if it gets too hot?" she asked.

"No, Kalin! I can't! It's on a timer! We can't control it!"

"Why not?"

"It's a central-heating building! That means that the heater turns on and off on its own schedule! If it stays cold out there, then this place will get extremely stuffy and dry!"

"Then open a window, Mike."

"Oh sure! Then we'll have a freezing cold draft blowing!"

"Look, I'm tired. I'm going to go to sleep." And with that she pulled the blanket around her and fell asleep.

I lay awake and stared at the heater. There was a clinking sound, a whirring sound, the heater began blowing dry, hot air into the bedroom. Clink, whirr, clink.

"It's beginning," I whispered to myself. "God help us."

As the dry, stuffy, hot air began to invade the room, I felt a droplet of sweat forming on my forehead. I pulled the covers away from my body and walked over to the fan in the corner of our room and turned it on. At first, the fan turned the air cooler and I felt a pang of relief, but in short order the heater intercepted the cool air and turned it stuffy and hot again. Now the droplet of sweat on my forehead had turned into many droplets of sweat, and it wasn't only my forehead. There were now droplets of sweat on my legs, my arms, my back, and in my butt crack, and on my balls too.

I pressed Save and sent it to Ben. An hour later he wrote back. He said that he'd read what I wrote about how stuffy the apartment gets and about how my butt crack and balls get sweaty and then he said he'd prefer that I try to be more creative. I said that I didn't have it in me to write "creative nonfiction" because I'm not from San Francisco. He said that wasn't true. He said that San Francisco had nothing to do with it. I said we'd have to agree to disagree. He said that it wasn't subjective. I said that I didn't know what the word *subjective* meant and that Rice-A-Roni is from San Francisco and that if he wanted to dispute *that* he'd lose in a court of law. He seemed confused.

My Morning Routine, #6

- Does anyone actually eat rum raisin–flavored ice cream?

- Instead of a string quartet what if there was a string *bean* quartet? How crazy would that be?

- It's always embarrassing when I take my car to the shop because when they tell me that something is wrong with my "struts" I tell them that they are wrong and then I strut around to prove it.

- I hate those guys who carry dog-eared classic novels around in their coat pockets everywhere they go. They just do it so that people will know they read. Who cares?

- They tend to be the same guys who show up at a party or a dinner with unopened FedEx packages with "scripts" in them. Couldn't they have just left the FedEx package at home? It's their way of saying, "People send me FedEx packages with scripts in them." Who cares?

- I have noticed that if the temperature falls below 65 degrees in Los Angeles, everyone puts on down coats, scarves, and winter hats. When I'm there I want to fit in, but it goes against everything I believe to wear a down coat when it's only 62 degrees outside.

How to Write and Sell
a Hollywood Screenplay

Chapter Three

DEVISE A PLOT

First and foremost, in order to write your own screenplay, you will need to have a great PLOT.

Q: **What is a plot?**
Good question. A plot is a story. It's what happens.

Q: **What's a story?**
A story is an account of an event with a beginning, middle, and end. As an exercise I want you to think of a story that happened to you. It can be anything you want. It could even be a story about what you ate for lunch today.

Q: **Cubano pork sandwich.**
Terrific! Tell this story to a friend, and if you don't have any friends, tell it to a stranger on the street or just talk to yourself. Did it have a beginning, a middle, and an end? If so, that was a story! And a story is a plot! Way to go! You're 83 percent finished! All you need to do now is write it up and sell it.

Q: **I'm still confused. All I said was "Cubano pork sandwich."**
Perfect question! Sprucing up the story is very important. And
here's how you do it: *Shit needs to get all fucked up in the middle.*

Q: **Huh? I didn't ask a question. I made a statement.**
Uh-huh. Let us examine a classic film: *Chinatown*. This is
widely considered to be a perfect screenplay. Why? Because shit
gets all fucked up in the middle. Let's take a look at the plot.
There's a guy, shit gets all fucked up in the middle, and then it
ends. If shit didn't get all fucked up in the middle, then it would
have been a really boring movie. Right?

Q: **Okay, but *Chinatown* is a criminal thriller! All *I* did was eat
a Cubano pork sandwich. How can shit get fucked up with a
sandwich?**
Maybe your sandwich turns into a monster! Maybe you and
your sandwich fall in love, then break up! Maybe your sandwich
contracts a fatal illness and dies? There are so many ways for
your story to get fucked up in the middle.

Q: **Yeah. Now I see.**
Let's review: Everything is normal, shit gets fucked up in the
middle, and then it ends. That is the plot of every movie ever
made.

Q: **Okay, but let's say that I just want to write a chick flick. Can
shit still get all fucked up in the middle?**
Absolutely! It can be fucked up but in a cute way. Let's take a
look at an ensemble chick flick comedy to see if the formula
still exists: *The Sisterhood of the Traveling Pants*. Certainly that
movie is nothing like *Chinatown*. It's about a pair of magic
pants, for fuck's sake. But upon closer inspection we discover
that perhaps this is not true. What's the plot of *Sisterhood of the
Traveling Pants*? In the beginning it's about a bunch of young

girls with a magic pair of pants, but then shit gets fucked up: Will Eric break Bee's heart? Will Lena listen to her heart or will her grandparents break her and the Greek dude apart? Will Carmen be strong enough to embrace her new family? Will Tibby's friend Bailey die of cancer? In other words, it's fucked up in the middle, and then the movie ends.

Q: **Wow. You're right! I just wish I had a plot to write a movie about. Harrumph.**
Having trouble devising a plot? No worries. Here's a ready-made plot for you. All you've got to do is fill in the blanks!

ROMANTIC COMEDY PLOT

There's this young woman named _____ (*insert boy's name and add "ie" to the end*). She has a very good job working at a _____ (*insert creative job in corporate setting with lots of gay coworkers*). She is lonely. We know she's lonely because she talks to her _____ (*insert breed of animal capable of facial expressions*) named _____ (*insert famous painter's last name*) about how she wants to meet a man.

Even though she's really beautiful, we learn that she's really just a normal gal. We learn this because she eats _____ (*insert type of junk food*) at night while watching _____ (*insert name of famous sad movie*). And also she _____ (*clumsy act involving her jeans*) while getting ready for work in the morning.

Things get interesting when she meets a handsome business executive named _____ (*type of tool*) who works for the company that is trying to merge with her company. They have instant karma and we know this because when their eyes meet a really cool and memorable song plays on the soundtrack by _____ (*insert name of song by the Postal Service*).

Things get even more interesting when she's on the street and she literally bumps into a really good-looking guy named _____ (*insert any man's name that begins with the letter* J *except for Jerry*). "J" is a local guy. He has lived in the city his whole life. He has a good job working as a _____ (*type of job where interacting with kind elderly people is likely*).

She starts dating both men and weighs their pros and cons. She really likes J because he took her to an adorable _____ (*type of ethnic restaurant*) that was off the beaten path. She likes the business executive because he took her to a _____ (*type of sporting event*) and had box seats. She likes J because after dinner he took her to a special hidden spot that no one else knows about near the _____ (*name of bridge*) with an amazing view of the stars and told her a story about _____ (*type of constellation*). She likes the business executive because after their gala event he took her back to his hotel room and _____ (*vulgar word for "had sex with"*) her brains out. And also she likes the business executive because he has _____ (*number between six and twelve*) -pack abs. She also likes the businessman because he's hung like a _____ (*type of large mammal*).

We know that she should choose J because in a pivotal scene he understands her _____ (*insert sad story about losing a grandparent*) in a way that no one else does. He also surprises her, in a good way, when he gets angry at her for implying that just because he _____ (*insert reason for thinking that someone is uneducated*) doesn't mean that he isn't smart; and that just because he _____ (*insert reason for thinking that someone doesn't make a lot of money*) doesn't mean that he can't make her happy; and that just because he _____ (*insert reason for thinking that someone isn't cultured*) doesn't mean that he's not cultured. Most importantly, we know that he is right for her because the actor playing J, _____ (*insert name of famous film actor*), is more famous than _____ (*insert name of hunky TV actor*), the actor playing the business executive.

At the end of the movie she's about to marry the business executive. Meanwhile, J is about to get on a _____ (*insert type of transportation vehicle*) and our heroine realizes that she should be with him because she's passing through town with the business executive and looks into a store window and sees _____ (*insert cute knickknack object that she and*

J made jokes about earlier in the movie). She tries to make the same joke with the business executive but he doesn't get it.

She races to the _____ (*insert place where transportation vehicle is*) and finds J just as he is about to get on the _____ (*insert same type of transportation vehicle. One good suggestion would be "airplane"*). She makes an impassioned speech, telling J that she's realized that his faults are really what she loves about him the most. J is suspicious at first but then she says, "Without you I'm _____ (*insert sentence that describes misery and loneliness*)." This convinces J that she's for real and they kiss. An old woman who has been watching all of this says _____ (*insert raunchy but cute joke*). The end. Credits roll while _____ (*insert Norah Jones song title*) plays followed by blooper scenes of the actors' hilarious on-set hijinks between takes. Congratulations! You just wrote your first screenplay treatment!

How to Write and Sell
a Hollywood Screenplay

Chapter Four

TROUBLESHOOTING

Writing a screenplay is not easy. But here are some easy shortcuts that you can use to fix any plot problems that you encounter along the way.

1. *The Obscure Law That They Forgot to Change Is a Cure-All for Any Plot Contrivance*

Let's say you're writing a suspense/thriller and something in your story just does not make any sense. For example: Your main character is denied access to a haunted hotel room, the room where everyone in the movie stays just before they die. As the writer, it's important to keep your main character out of the room initially but also ensure that, at some point in the movie, he gains access. But how will he do it? Doesn't the hotel have the right to deny him this access if they so wish? It's their hotel, isn't it? And they don't want anyone else to die in there. Well, they don't have the right if there's "an obscure law that they forgot to change" that says that it's unlawful for a hotel to deny someone access to a room if the room is vacant *even if* the room is haunted and likely to murder its guest. See how that works? Not only have you fixed the problem but you've also got a great scene where your main character gets to dust off an old law book that they forgot about and stay up late reading it. Nota bene: It's of no importance that you explain who the *they* in "they forgot to change" is. Throw in the terms *municipal courts* and you'll be fine.

2. Standing in Front of the Mirror Practicing What You Will Say to Someone You Have a Crush on Is Very Endearing and Also Moves the Story Forward

Let's say your main character has feelings for his hot coworker but feels like she's "out of his league," but he's also not such a pussy that he doesn't have the balls to ask her out. I mean, he's intimidated by her, smitten, but he's also self-assured enough to ask her out; he's a man of action. If he weren't we'd like him less. How do we show all this duality in a short scene? Easy: Have him stand in front of the mirror and practice what he'll say to her when he asks her out. Have him try it in many different ways. Each way should be funny and offbeat. This scene lets you show us your main character's "inner life" in a funny, surprising, and entertaining way.

3. Security Guards Watch Sports on Small Portable Black-and-White Televisions and Are Easily Distracted by This, Which Allows Your Main Character to Sneak into the Room They Are Guarding

Your main character needs to gain access to a guarded room. How will he do this? Easy: The security guard isn't paying attention because he's watching sports on a portable television and isn't paying attention.

4. Microfiche Is Easy to Navigate and Readily Available at Every Public Library Nationwide

Your main character is suspicious about someone and wants to learn more about him. How will your main character do this? Easy: She goes to the public library and scans through microfiche. Everything she needs to learn will be easy to find. The great thing about microfiche is that it seems like your main character is working really hard to find this information because microfiche is a visual code word for "lots of research."

5. The Wrong Boyfriend Doesn't Like to Dance

You're writing a romantic comedy and you want the audience to know that your main female character is in a bad relationship. How do you show that in a quick way without needing to go into too much detail? Easy: He doesn't like to dance. This tells us that he's not spontaneous, adventurous, or romantic. As soon as the "right guy" asks her to dance, we'll know he's "the one."

6. All Computers Have the Ability to Zoom In on and Focus a Photograph No Matter How Blurry or Obscure, but It Could Take a While

Your main character has a photograph of the villain but it's very blurry. You'd like him to be able to discover the identity of the person in the photo, but you don't want it to be *too* easy. No problem: The computer can do it but it will take a while. This is good too because you can intermittently cut back to the computer lab and have your main character ask the computer technician how it's going and the computer technician can say, "It's going slowly. I need more time."

7. If You Want Your Movie to Be Taken Seriously, Put Catherine Keener in It

You're writing a "serious" film. It doesn't have to be a drama but you'd like it to be considered for festivals and eventually win awards. In order to do this, you must write a part for Catherine Keener. If you can't get Catherine Keener, then you're kind of screwed.

8. In Order to Defeat an Evil Spirit You Have to Scream at It

Let's say you're writing a horror movie about an evil spirit. You're near the end of your screenplay and there's only one character still alive. She's trapped inside the house with the evil spirit and is about to be killed. You want her to defeat the spirit but you're not sure how she's going to do that, considering the fact that we've already seen the evil spirit murder a lot of people. Here's how you do it: Have her scream at the evil spirit and tell the evil spirit that she's fed up. This will be the first time in the film that this character didn't act like a victim. The evil spirit will respond favorably to this.

9. The Cop's Wife Wants Him to Spend More Time at Home

If your main character is a cop and you're looking for a good subplot for him, then I suggest you make his wife want him to stay home more often. At some point, she tells him, "You have no idea what it's like to wonder if someone's calling to tell me that you're dead every time the phone rings."

10. The New Husband Is Wimpier Than Your Hero, but He's a Better Provider, and He's Also Tolerant of the Fact That Your Hero Still Comes Around a Lot

Your hero was never a good husband or a good father. That's your hero's cross to bear. He's good at other things, but he was never very stable. Now his ex-wife has a new husband. The new husband should be a bit of wimp, but it should be clear that he takes better care of your hero's ex-wife and kid than your hero ever did. Also, when your hero comes to the house to pick up his kids for visitation, he and the new husband should have a chilly but cordial relationship.

11. College Professors Lead Surprisingly Lively Debates with Their Students in Which They Discuss the Themes of the Movie Without Being Too Obvious About It

This is a good opportunity to highlight the themes of your film without the audience knowing it. For example: Let's say your movie involves questions of "The Afterlife." Have your main character be a college professor who teaches a class on "The Afterlife." This lets you kill many birds with one stone, because not only do we get to learn about your film's themes, we also get to see that the main character is good at his job, well-liked by his students, and looks great in a tweed coat.

12. *All High School Jocks Are Evil Unless They Have a Secret Talent That They Can't Tell Their Father About*

If you're writing a teen comedy or teen romance and you want to have a jock as the male lead, then he must secretly want to be either a painter, a dancer, or a poet, but his dad can't know about it. If his dad finds out, then he will lose his father's love. This endears us to the jock and makes him seem more "real" to us. If he has no secret talent, then he's just another evil jock and, therefore, can't be the lead.

My Morning Routine, #7

- There is no way to look cool while holding an ice cream cone.

- There is no way to look cool while riding a bicycle no-handed, unless you actually do not have any hands. If you do not have any hands, then it's actually very cool.

- I saw a documentary recently on PBS about the Donner Party. It was about a bunch of settlers in the 1800s who got stuck traveling west and wound up starving and freezing and eventually eating each other. Sounds like a pretty lame party.

- I really like walking up a hill but I really hate walking uphill.

- There's this show called *Mystery Diagnosis* on the Discovery Health channel. Every episode chronicles the true story of someone who is stricken with a mysterious illness but can't find a diagnosis. At the end of each story, they finally meet a doctor who is able to give them a diagnosis. It's like a TV show version of an Oliver Sacks book and the illnesses are genuinely mysterious. The episodes have intriguing names like "The Woman Whose Legs Turned Black," "The Boy Who Never Cried," and "The Man Who Couldn't Move." There was one episode called "The Girl with Half a Face." Basically, half of this poor twelve-year-old girl's face inexplicably caved in. Her mother took her to a thousand different doctors and none of them could diagnose her. Finally, she meets a doctor who is able to diagnose her with

Parry-Romberg Syndrome. The doctor gives a straight-to-camera testimonial and tells the interviewer that when he saw the girl he suspected that it might be Parry-Romberg Syndrome because the primary symptom of Parry-Romberg Syndrome is...that half of your face caves in. Gee, thanks, Doc.

Close-up Photographs of Your Face

In my parents' kitchen, just above the breakfast table, there's a wall of framed photos. It's mostly family snapshots: my sister and I doing handstands at Virginia Beach as kids, my parents standing arm in arm in front of various European art museums, my niece and nephew with ice cream on their faces. But there's one photo that stands out from the rest—my first professional headshot.

In layman's terms, headshots are 8½" × 11" unbelievably close-up photographs of your face. Practically speaking, a headshot is the aspiring young actor's calling card. Typically, the aspiring young actor will staple his or her résumé to the back of their headshot and then send it around to agents and casting directors in hopes of "being noticed."

In the picture, I am twenty-one years old, posing with my arms crossed and a little smirk on my face that says, "I'm a douche bag, please give me a job." Every time I visit home, I beg my mother to remove the picture, but she refuses. "You're so handsome in it," she says.

"I can't bear to look at it," I say.

"Noooo," she says. "You look very handsome."

"I don't look handsome, Mom! I look like a douche bag. Please take it down!" I plead.

"Absolutely not," she says. "You look very handsome. And stop saying 'douche bag'!"

I know *for a fact* that I look like a douche bag, but it's a battle that I will never win. When I look at the headshots, I don't see what she sees. She sees her son—I see a douche bag.

sitcom hair

eyes making love
to camera

smirk that says,
"The next James
Spader"

sensitive and
thoughtful
Art Garfunkel
vest

flowy shirt hiding
bulging muscles

My "acting career" began, in an unofficial capacity, in the third
grade. I got into it for a girl. She lived on the corner of my street. Her
name was Karen. She was preppy with an olive-colored complexion and
dark brown hair and eyes. She looked like Anne Frank in an L.L. Bean
sweater. I had a big crush on her.

I created an elaborate fantasy that she had installed video surveillance cameras in my bedroom and was watching my every move. I am
very forward thinking. Before MTV's *The Real World* or any concept
of reality TV ever existed, I am starring in my own personal reality TV
show with an audience of one.

I "act cool" alone in my room for her. At that age, acting "cool"
means acting like Danny Zuko from *Grease*. I strut around my room
with my sleeves rolled up above my shoulders, I flex my nonexistent

muscles, strike dramatic "pelvis-y" poses, and I occasionally break into song—"Greased Lightning" sung in a ten-year-old's high tenor.

When I see Karen in school, I expect her to bring up my little performances. "Hey, Mike, I really liked that showstopping number you did last night before you went to bed."

I'd be like, "Oh, you saw that?"

And then she'd say, "Yes. I'm watching your every move with the surveillance cameras that I had installed in your house."

But it never happened. In retrospect, I'm thinking she had no surveillance cameras.

Cut to: Los Angeles, March 1996. 10:00 a.m. I am in Los Angeles for "pilot season." I have an audition for the "Untitled Steve Levitan Project." The character is described as "Twentysomething, smart, funny, David Schwimmer–type." I go to the audition and sit in a room filled with twenty "*mes.*" We are all carbon copies of each other: twentysomething, smart, funny, David Schwimmer–types wearing pressed jeans and running our fingers through our thick "sitcom hair." I feel like I'm in a Stanley Kubrick movie. I'm freaked out and begin to think that maybe I am a robot. I tank the audition.

After sixth grade, I go to Camp Mohawk in the Berkshires and begin my "legitimate" acting career. The camp is tiny, only forty campers, and while their brochure offers many sports, the only sport anyone ever plays is ping-pong. Mostly we just hang around and sing Billy Joel songs at the top of our lungs.

I audition for their big summer production of *Oliver!* I am really hoping for the role of the Artful Dodger. My parents have the album from the original London production, and I know all of the lines by heart. "Consider yourself at home! Consider yourself one of the family! We've taken to you so strong! It's clear we're going to get along!"

I don't get cast as the Artful Dodger. I get cast as Fagin. Fagin is the leader of the pickpocket gang. He is described in Charles Dickens's book *Oliver Twist* as being "disgusting" to look at. This doesn't work wonders for my ego, but still, I am up for the challenge. And it *is* a challenge. I am twelve years old and Fagin is an old man. In order to play Fagin, I will need to "become" an old man. I do this by:

a) "Hunching" over
b) Walking slowly
c) Talking with a "raspy, growly voice"

Cut to: Los Angeles, February 2001. 1:00 p.m. Audition for another "Untitled Steve Levitan Project." Steve Levitan has an "untitled" project every year. I am reading for the part of Office Intern. He is described as being "nineteen years old." I am thirty-one years old. I call my agent and tell him that I'm too old for the part. He tells me not to worry and that "they're not sure what they are looking for." When I go to the audition, the waiting room is filled with nineteen-year-old boys. I sense that in fact they *do* know what they are looking for. I sign my name on the call sheet. When I am brought into the room for my audition, the casting director pulls me aside and politely tells me that I am "too old" for the part.

My senior year in high school, I get cast as Judge Hathorne in our winter production of Arthur Miller's *The Crucible*. Judge Hathorne is, by all accounts, a small role. Judge Danforth is the meatier judge part. By meatier, I mean that he has more lines than Judge Hathorne, and I know this because as soon as I get the part, I go through the script and count my lines. I also count Judge Danforth's lines and I deduce that Danforth has four times more lines then Judge Hathorne. Still, all my life, I've been hearing the saying "There are no small parts, only small actors." I am determined to make the most of it.

One day in rehearsal for *The Crucible*, we are practicing a particularly heated argument between John Proctor and Judge Danforth. While Danforth and Proctor have it out in the center stage, my character stands off to the side, listening.

As the two leads argue, I wonder, "How does my character *feel* about this argument?" I think, "He's angry! He's really angry!" A voice inside my head says, "ACT!" So I let out an audible "Arrghhh!" It feels really good. I AM BECOMING JUDGE HATHORNE. I start stomping around, exclaiming "Arrghh!" and wildly gesticulating my arms until, from somewhere in the theater, I hear the director yell, "STOP!" We all stop.

"Michael," he says.

"Yes?" I say, a little out of breath.

"What are you doing?" he asks, twirling his beard hair with his thumb and forefinger.

The actors playing Proctor and Danforth use this time to catch their breath, because they're winded from having so many lines and so many different emotions to play.

"What do you mean?" I say.

"What's with all the flailing around?" he continues.

"I'm angry," I say.

"Uh-huh," he says, thinking. He's loosening his turtleneck now. I can tell he's upset.

"I'm upset because John Proctor is making me angry," I say. "I think that Goody Osburn is a witch, and I want to drown her."

"Uh-huh. Well, please stop doing that," he says.

"Why?" I ask, confused.

"Because you're pulling focus," he says.

"Oh," I say. "What does that mean?"

"It *means* you're drawing attention away from what's important," he says impatiently. "Okay, guys, let's start from the top of the scene. Showalter, this time, please just stay on the stool and take quiet notes with your quill pen like we discussed."

"Okay," I say. Then I put my pilgrim hat back on, and do what I'm told for the rest of the play. I don't want to draw attention away from what's important. No small parts.

Cut to: Los Angeles, May 2005. 4:00 p.m. "General meeting" with major film studio executive.

I wait in the lobby for an hour and a half.

The executive's assistant is a good-looking recent graduate of Duke University named Nils.

He offers me water every twenty minutes.

At 5:30 p.m. the executive emerges. He is younger than me and wears a denim shirt.

He apologizes for making me wait.

We shake hands.

He brings me into his office and asks me to sit down.

I sit.

He shows me his framed poster of an old Orson Welles movie. He tells me he's a huge film purist, then tells me that he's working on a movie about a bunch of teenagers trying to get laid.

He tells me that it's "testing off the charts." I don't know what this means.

I have barely opened my mouth. He tells me that he is a huge fan of Paul Rudd and is trying to find a film project for them to work on together.

I agree with him that Paul is very funny and talented.

"Tell me about you!" he says. "I don't know anything about you."

I try to talk about myself. I tell him that I have an idea to pitch.

He rubs his hands together enthusiastically and says, "Great. Let's hear it!"

I start talking, "It's a romantic comedy about a guy who's never been dumped. He's always the one who does the—"

"Paul's sense of humor is brilliant," he interjects. "We love him here."

"Uh-huh," I say.

"I have a script that I'm dying for him to rewrite and star in."

"Cool," I say.

"He's reading it this weekend."

"That's great. I hope he likes it," I say.

"Me too. Fingers crossed."

"Yeah. So anyway, the guy has never been dum—"

"Would you mind putting in a good word with Paul for me?"

"Sure," I say.

"Great," he says. "So, you were saying…it's about a guy who gets dumped?"

"Uh. No. He's actually never been dumped—"

"Even better!" he says.

"Yeah, so—"

"You know Ben Stiller, right?" he asks.

"Not that well," I say.

"He's brilliant," he says.

"I agree," I say.

"I'm working on a project with him right now. It's going to be big."

I nod and listen. He finishes telling me about the project he and Ben Stiller are working on together and then begins to tell me about another project he and Ben Stiller already worked on together.

I nod and listen.

Now he tells me about a third project they worked on together.

I am starting to go into a dissociative fugue.

Now he's talking to me about Rowan Atkinson.

I'm not that familiar with his work.

He's telling me how much he loves Rowan Atkinson and would I put in a good word with Rowan if I ever see him.

I smile and nod and tap my foot.

He wants to know if I know Zach Galifianakis.

He wants to know if I can call Will Arnett on his behalf and put in a good word regarding a script they've sent him.

Now he's asking me for Will Ferrell's contact info.

He says he has John Cleese in mind for a part.

He wants to know do I know John Cleese? I say no.

He wants to know what my relationship is like with Steve Martin and could I put in a good word.

Now he's taking a call.

Now he's making an evening plan with his wife.

Now he's standing up and thanking me for meeting with him.

We shake hands.

I leave.

One of the first things you learn as an aspiring young actor is the importance of "getting an agent." "Getting an agent" is that first big step
toward success, a sign that you are better than your peers who do not
have "an agent." Shortly before graduating from college, I acquired a
dog-eared how-to book for breaking into the business called *Audition*.
It was a slim yellow volume for aspiring young thespians. It had chapter
headings like:

- Chapter One: How to make a great first impression
- Chapter Four: How to make a great second impression
- Chapter Seven: How to make your third impression feel like a
  first impression

The book said one good way to "get an agent" is to ask a friend who
already has an "agent" if he will introduce you to his "agent" and help
you "set up a meeting." At this "meeting," you can charm the "agent,"
get "signed," and brag to your friends about your "agent" at parties.
Being "signed" means that you and your "agent" have put your partner-
ship in writing. If it's not in writing, then you can't brag about it.

Golden Rule: Never refer to your agent by his/her actual name.
Always call them "my agent." Example: "I can't go to your birthday
party next weekend because 'my agent' and I are going to a hockey
game." Notice how much less impressive this statement is if you refer
to your agent by his or her name: "I can't go to your birthday party
next weekend because Linda and I are going to a hockey game." If your
friends don't know that "Linda" is your agent, then there's no point in
telling the story.

Cut to: Los Angeles, May 2007.

I have a 3:30 p.m. meeting at Universal Studios in Burbank. It's a
very important meeting. I cannot be late. I need to appear very respon-

sible and professional. First impressions are everything. Burbank is a maze. Thank God I paid extra for GPS in the rental car, otherwise I'd never find it. I go where the GPS tells me to go.

3:17 p.m. There is traffic on the 101. I'm getting nervous. I think I will be okay, though. GPS says, "Go north on 101 to Barham Boulevard." I take the exit on Barham Boulevard. Make right into Universal Studios.

3:23 p.m. Directions take me to *Jurassic Park* ride entrance.

Security guard tells me that I am nowhere near where I am supposed to be.

Guard tells me to make a U-turn.

3:28 p.m. I get back on 101 North.

Take Lankershim Boulevard exit.

Make right into Universal Studios.

I am now going to be late for my meeting. FUCK!!!

I follow directions.

New directions also take me to *Jurassic Park* ride entrance. It's just a different entrance.

It is now 3:42. I'm currently twelve minutes late. If I can make it there in three minutes, I'm still within an acceptable window of lateness that I can attribute to "traffic."

I can also break out the old "I'm a New Yorker and get lost here easily."

That's such a wimp out, though. Damn it.

Guard tells me to make U-turn, go back on Lankershim Boulevard, make right on Main Street, and another right into Universal Studios.

3:47 p.m. I make a right on Lankershim, a right on Main Street, and a right into Universal Studios. I'm really late now. And having a panic attack. Chest is stiffening. Shortness of breath. Dizziness. Nausea. Diarrhea is a real possibility.

I keep following directions.

New directions take me to right place.

Guard at gate tells me to make U-turn and use parking lot on the right.

I make U-turn and follow directions to parking lot on the right.

Guard inside parking lot tells me to make U-turn into visitor parking on the right.

It's my fifth fucking U-turn!

It is now 3:51. I have officially passed the window of acceptable lateness. Thirty minutes late is a death knell. Now I'm going to have to come up with an excuse.

I run through some possibilities in my mind.

1. Pretend I thought the meeting was at 4:00 p.m. and feign surprise when I discover it was really 3:30.
2. Blame the misunderstanding on my agent. Tell them he's got a drinking problem and that "we're all really worried about him."
3. Claim my previous meeting had run long. This would have the side benefit of making it seem like I am "in demand." On the flip side, I want them to feel special, like they're "the only one."

Shit! I was so busy thinking up excuses that I missed the U-turn.

4:01 p.m. I make U-turn and park in visitor parking.

Inside lobby, a guard tells me to take elevator to fourth floor.

4:04 p.m. I get out on the fourth floor. Guard on fourth floor tells me to take different elevator to the eighth floor.

4:10 p.m. I am on eighth floor. I wait in the lobby.

I tell receptionist that I am there.

She tells me that the executive I am meeting is "running late" for the meeting, and can she get me a bottle of water while I wait?

Cut to: New York City, 1992. My friend Sam, who had graduated from college a year before me, had moved to New York City to pursue an acting career. He immediately "got an agent" at a "boutique agency" that represented "hip young New York actors." Sam told his agent, Scott, about me and helped me "set up a meeting." I was thrilled. I knew that when Sam's agent met me he would want to sign me. He'd see me and think, "Sean Penn but funny."

On the day of my big meeting with Scott, I decided to wear the exact same "outfit" that I wore in my headshot. It was my coolest look, and I didn't want to leave anything to chance.

9:30 a.m.: I arrive at Penn Station via New Jersey Transit train, and although I am more than an hour early for my meeting, I go straight to the agency, because the book emphasized that you should "never be late for a meeting."

9:45 a.m.: I sign in with the receptionist, a pretty, blond woman. She is the kind of girl who would have never paid attention to me in high school other than to cheat off my tests, which would have been futile, because I would have been trying to cheat off her too.

9:50 a.m.: If I didn't know it was a talent agency, I might think this is a yoga center. The lobby is sparse, clean, and spacious, with glass offices and nice leather couches. Against the wall there is a small rock garden with water trickling over it. It reminds me of the time I went to a yoga class with my girlfriend. The instructor told us, in a voice so calm it made me panic, "Okay, breathe, now relax your head, your ears, your eyes, your nose, your mouth, now breathe, relax your arms, your shoulders, your hands, your tummy..." I was laying on the mat thinking, "Is she going to say 'relax your anus'? Please don't say 'relax your anus.'" Then she said, "Relax your pelvis, your waist, and your anus." I couldn't take it.

10:10 a.m.: A good-looking man in a business suit, no tie, pops his head through the glass doors and looks me up and down, his eyes darting back and forth between my head and my feet. He dashes back into the offices and closes the glass doors behind him.

11:00 a.m.: My meeting was scheduled for 11 a.m. 11 a.m. comes and goes without fanfare. I wait.

11:15 a.m.: I ask the receptionist to remind Scott that I am there waiting for him. She tells me he knows that I am waiting, that he is on a "conference call," and that he'll be with me shortly. (I have since learned that anytime anyone tells you they're on a "conference call," they're lying.)

11:30 a.m.: I notice the receptionist talking to someone on the lobby phone. She is looking at me, and I could swear I hear her say, every so quietly, "Oh my God, he's *still* here. Loser."

11:45 a.m.: I remind the receptionist for the third time that I have an 11 a.m. meeting with Scott, and she assures me that he will see me as soon as he is "off his conference call."

12:00 noon: I begin to feel like a piece of shit.

12:15 p.m.: The receptionist stands up and says, "Scott will see you now." The glass doors separating the lobby from the offices open and Scott appears. Scott, of course, is the same man who had "sized me up" one hour and forty minutes earlier. "Hey, Mike, sorry for the delay," he says, not making eye contact. "Come in."

12:20 p.m.: He leads me through the glass doors and into his office. It's a corner office with large picture windows and French film posters from the Sixties lining the walls. He is clearly an important player. "Please, sit down," he says.

"Thanks," I say.

"So," he says, "you know Sam?"

"Yes, Sam and I—"

"Isn't Sam amazing?" he interrupted.

"Yes," I say. Then I try to bring it back to me. The book says to talk about yourself. "Sam and I—"

"Sam just got cast in a play! He's really going places," he said.

"I know, I hea—"

"Do you have a headshot?" he asks.

I take the headshot out of a crisp manila envelope and I slide it across Scott's desk.

He picks it up and looks at it for what can't be much longer than a millisecond. He slides the headshot back to me and says, "Michael, you're not what we're looking for."

"Uh-huh," I respond. I am not prepared for this. I try to remember if there is a chapter in the book called "What to Do in the Face of Cruel Rejection."

"We have a bunch of young, funny white guys already," he says.

"Good luck to you." Pause. I sit there in my white jeans and Art Garfunkel vest, staring at him.

"Do you even want to see a monologue?" I say. "I've prepared the Tom monologue from *The Glass Menager—*"

"Nope, don't need to," he says as he stands and offers me his hand. "If you're ever in something, let us know. We'll come check it out."

"Thanks, I will," I say. "I definitely will."

He points me to the door.

I walk back through the corridors of the agency alone. My white jeans make a crunchy sound as I walk. I say good-bye to the receptionist on my way to the elevator. She doesn't respond. I wobble out onto the street, make my way back to Penn Station, and take the train home to New Jersey.

Back at home, my parents are eager to hear about my day.

"How did it go?" they ask.

"Good," I lie. "He wants to come to see me in something."

"That's great," they say.

"Yes," I say. "It's really great."

"Did he like the headshot?" my mom asks.

"Yes, he loved it."

"Of course he did," she says. "It's such a handsome picture."

Cut to: Los Angeles, October 2009. 11:30 a.m. "General meeting" with major TV network. A "general meeting" is a meeting that is about "nothing in general." Or, "generally speaking," the meeting has no purpose. I am there to "get to know people."

A young woman enters the lobby and looks directly at me. I smile at her. She seems perplexed.

"Are you Michael?" she asks.

"Yes," I say.

"Really? I didn't recognize you," she says.

"Huh," I say. "Why?"

"You look very different in real life."

"Really?" I say. "I think I look the same."

"Yes, maybe it's just from the side, though."

"Maybe you were expecting Michael Ian Black?"

"Oh no! I *know* what he looks like!" Then she corrects herself, "I mean, I know what you look like too."

"Yeah, but you didn't recognize me," I say.

"Not from the side, no." She laughs.

She guides me into an office where I am greeted by two women and one man.

When I enter they all rise. We shake hands.

"Wow. You look really different in real life," says the main woman executive.

"That's what she said," I say, pointing to the young woman who brought me into the room.

"Yeah. I said that to him and he got defensive," the young woman tells the main executive.

"I think she thought I was Michael Ian Black," I say.

"Oh no. We know you're not Michael Ian Black," says the woman executive. "We know what he looks like. It's just that you look smaller in real life."

"Smaller?" I ask.

"Yes," she says. "You look smaller and more petite. But that's in no way an insult."

The man in the room rolls his eyes and says, "You just insulted him."

"No, the opposite. It's a compliment. He looks huskier on the TV show."

"You just insulted him again," says the man.

"No!" says the woman executive. "I *wish* someone would say that I'm petite." She is undeniably extremely petite.

"You are very petite," I say.

"You just look taller on TV, that's all," she says.

The meeting is less than five minutes old.

A Never-Ending Sketch

INT. CONFERENCE ROOM—RAZOR BLADE COMPANY—DAY

A GROUP OF EXECUTIVES in business attire sits around a conference table. In front of each EXEC is a dossier of papers. The PRESIDENT of the company addresses them.

PRESIDENT: Hey, everyone, it's time to put out a "new and improved" razor for the fall season. We've had our Ultra 3 on the market for a few years now, it's a big seller, but it's time for a change! Suggestions?

Murmurs in the boardroom. Finally, a YOUNG EXEC raises his hand.

YOUNG EXEC: What about an extra blade?

PRESIDENT: An extra blade?

YOUNG EXEC: I know it's a crazy idea but it seemed to work when we went from the Ultra to the Ultra 2, and then again when we went from the Ultra 2 to the Ultra 3.

PRESIDENT: What will we call this one?

Murmurs. An OLDER EXEC raises his hand.

OLDER EXEC: May I suggest "Ultra 4"?

PRESIDENT: Hm. "Ultra 4." I like it. I like it a lot. So we're adding an extra blade, are we?

Murmurs.

PRESIDENT: All in favor?

EXECUTIVES all say "aye."

PRESIDENT: All opposed?

No one says anything.

PRESIDENT: Meeting adjourned!

Everyone gets up, shakes hands, and walks out of the boardroom.

GRAPHIC: "Two years later."

INT. SAME CONFERENCE ROOM—RAZOR BLADE COMPANY—DAY

The same GROUP OF EXECUTIVES in business attire sits around a conference table. The PRESIDENT of the company addresses them.

PRESIDENT: Hey, everyone, it's time to put out a "new and improved" razor for the fall season. We've had our Ultra 4 on the market for a few years now, it's a big seller, but it's time for a change! Suggestions?

Murmurs in the boardroom. Finally, a YOUNG EXEC raises his hand.

YOUNG EXEC: What about an extra blade?

PRESIDENT: An extra blade?

YOUNG EXEC: I know it's a crazy idea but it seemed to work when we went from the Ultra to the Ultra 2, and then again when we went from the Ultra 2 to the Ultra 3, and then again when we went from the Ultra 3 to the Ultra 4.

PRESIDENT: What will we call this one?

Murmurs. An OLDER EXEC raises his hand.

OLDER EXEC: May I suggest "Ultra 5"?

PRESIDENT: Hm. "Ultra 5." I like it. I like it a lot. So we're adding an extra blade, are we?

Murmurs.

PRESIDENT: All in favor?

EXECUTIVES all say "aye."

PRESIDENT: All opposed?

No one says anything.

PRESIDENT: Meeting adjourned!

Everyone gets up, shakes hands, and walks out of the boardroom.

GRAPHIC: "One Hundred Years Later."

INT. CONFERENCE ROOM—RAZOR BLADE COMPANY—DAY

A GROUP OF EXECUTIVES in futuristic business attire sits around a futuristic conference table. In front of each EXEC is a computer. The PRESIDENT of the company addresses them.

PRESIDENT: Hey, everyone, it's time to put out a "new and improved" razor for the fall season. We've had our "Ultra 65" on the market for a few years now, it's a big seller, but it's time for a change! Suggestions?

Murmurs in the boardroom. Finally, a YOUNG EXEC raises his hand.

YOUNG EXEC: What about an extra blade?

PRESIDENT: An extra blade? Sixty-five blades isn't enough?

YOUNG EXEC: I know it's a crazy idea but it seemed to work when we went from the Ultra 63 to the Ultra 64, and then again when we went from the Ultra 64 to the Ultra 65.

PRESIDENT: What will we call this one?

Murmurs. An OLDER EXEC raises his hand.

OLDER EXEC: May I suggest "Millions of Blades"?

PRESIDENT: Very funny, Hankerstein. Very funny.

OLDER EXEC: Okay. Okay. How about "Ultra 66"?

PRESIDENT: Hm. "Ultra 66." I like it. I like it a lot. So we're adding an extra blade, are we?

Murmurs.

PRESIDENT: All in favor?

EXECUTIVES all say "aye."

PRESIDENT: All opposed?

No one says anything.

PRESIDENT: Meeting adjourned!

Everyone gets up, shakes hands, and walks out of the board-room.

GRAPHIC: "One thousand years later."

INT. CONFERENCE ROOM—RAZOR BLADE COMPANY—POSTAPOCALYPSE

A GROUP OF EXECUTIVES in postapocalyptic business attire sits around a conference table. In front of each EXEC is a parchment. The PRESIDENT of the company addresses them.

PRESIDENT: Hey, everyone, it's time to put out a "new and improved" razor for the fall season. We've had our Sharp Rock Razor Blade on the market for a few years now, it's big on the barter market, but it's time for a change! Suggestions?

Murmurs in the boardroom. Finally, a YOUNG EXEC raises his hand.

YOUNG EXEC: What about a "Sharp Rock with a Wooden Handle Attached"?

PRESIDENT: Who'll carve the wood?

FEMALE EXEC: No one. We will just use sticks.

YOUNG EXEC: I know it's a crazy idea but it seemed to work when, after the apocalypse, we went from the Ultra 878 to the Jagged Rock, and then again when we went from the Jagged Rock to the Sharp Rock.

PRESIDENT: Fair enough. What will we call this one?

Murmurs. An OLDER EXEC raises his hand.

OLDER EXEC: May I suggest "The Ultra"?

PRESIDENT: Hm. "The Ultra." I like it. I like it a lot. So we're adding a handle to the sharp rock, are we?

Murmurs.

PRESIDENT: All in favor?

EXECUTIVES all say "aye."

PRESIDENT: All opposed?

No one says anything.

PRESIDENT: Meeting adjourned!

Everyone gets up, shakes hands, and walks out of the board-room.

AND SO ON... the end.

Just Before the Author's Afterword

This section of my book is called Just Before the Author's Afterword. It's another of my book innovations. This section is meant to allow the reader to decompress a bit, take it all in, and catch his breath before dealing with the stress of reading the Author's Afterword, which will indicate that the book is over and that it's time to get on with the business of living your life. Here're a few things for you to visualize that will help you come down from the reading experience you've just had:

The sound of a babbling brook
Crickets quietly chirping late at night
The soothing hum of a fan
Valium
A really good Jack Johnson song
Morphine (snorted)
A cat purring

Good. Relax. Okay, the section Just Before the Author's Afterword has concluded. You are now ready to read the Author's Afterword.

Just After Just Before the Author's Afterword

But before we get to that I would like to just reflect a bit on this experience.

(Reflecting, reflecting, reflecting, reflecting)

If only you could see me reflecting right now. I'm really deep in thought.

(Reflecting, reflecting, reflecting, reflecting)

Okay, that was intense.

Author's Afterword

This book was really hard to write but it was an amazing journey. I fell WAY SHORT of my goal to write a profound and meaningful memoir. On that level I FAILED COMPLETELY. I did however manage to use the word *penis* over four hundred times. Do I regret that, instead of writing an accomplished and searing work of nonfiction, I wrote what basically amounts to a random string of unconnected and incoherent thoughts primarily on my cats? It's not an easy question to answer. And the reason it's not an easy question to answer is that I had a tooth removed this morning and I'm still groggy from the sleepy gas, so I'm not thinking very clearly.

I've decided that "important memoirs" are for people who've had "interesting lives" and who are "good writers." I can claim neither of those things and that's okay. If everybody had an "interesting" story to tell, then we'd be all be "interesting" and wouldn't that suck? Without boring people like me the interesting people wouldn't stand out! To the interesting people out there—you're welcome.

Here's the reality: I had a nervous breakdown trying to write this book, and though my writer's block landed me in the psych ward at Bellevue, I still pushed through and now consider those four months in lockup to have been an amazing growth experience—and I mean literally a growth experience. I am now a 9' 7" giant.

Without all the help I received from the doctors and nurses at Bellevue, I might still be running around in that bog, playing banjo with all my clothes off. I now know with total certainty that the FBI does not have a surveillance camera inside my tote bag, and I also know that my cat is not a space alien instructing me to build a potato chip replica of the Eiffel Tower in my backyard.

In no particular order I need to thank these people for helping me through that tough time: Dr. Melvin Shnitzler, Nurse Penny Poopy, Nurse Dina Vaducci, Dr. Ivar Stromley, Dr. Kate Stumplebutt, Nurse Dan Doodybutt, all the neurologists at Neurology Central, Dr. Barton Dickflapp, Dr. Wilhemina Wonderpooper, and Nurse Matt Shat. I also need to thank the great state of Vermont for donating so many potato chips to my cause. Hey, guys, I'm sorry I never finished the job.

Also, not in this volume is the five-hundred-page chapter entitled "The Limitless Potential of Wordless Pages," which was conceived during a manic episode. My editor, Ben, urged me not to include it in the book. He said, "Michael, it's five hundred blank pages. You can't do that. It's just a big waste of paper." And I said, "You need to think outside the box. If people keep reading the blank, wordless pages, then they will start to write their OWN book. In their minds." In the end, we decided not to include it in the book. Ultimately, I couldn't argue that it wasn't kind of "bullshitty."

In conclusion: The journey's the reward.

Thank you for spending this time with me.

Love and muffins,
Michael Showalter

Appendix

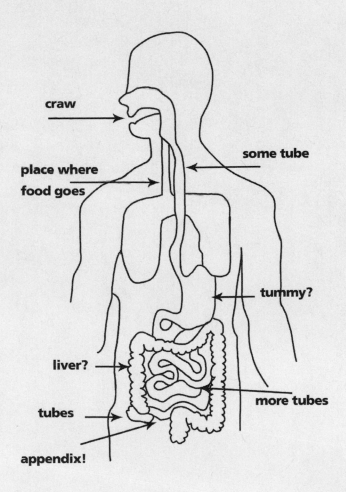

craw

some tube

place where
food goes

tummy?

liver?

more tubes

tubes

appendix!

Upcoming Books by the Author

(An excerpt from my journalistic novel that chronicles the championship Lakers of the 2000 season, called *A Season to Remember: Life on the Road in the NBA with Shaq, Kobe, and the Rest of the Guys on the Team*)

Day 1. Meeting the team. The guys seem cool about having me around. I can already tell that they've accepted me into the fold. Shaq in particular seems to have taken quite a shine to me. We bonded over the fact that we both like R.E.M.'s early albums the best. His personal fav is *Murmur*. Mine is *Document*. We'll deal. I can tell that he and I will be good friends by the time that this whole experience is over.

Day 2. The team had its first practice today. During a water break, I told Shaq that I thought he was dragging it a bit on the court and he seemed to take my note to heart. I told him that he looked like "a cow out there" and that if he wanted to make the all-star team he'd better "pick his fat butt up off the court and snap it back on or else he'd be lucky to get a job handing out towels to the other players." He took my criticism in stride and laughed it off. But I told him that I wasn't kidding and then reiterated to him about how I thought he looked like a "cow" and then I said "fuck you for not taking me seriously." Shaq was cool about it and apologized for not taking me seriously. It was a bullshit apology but I accepted it anyway because I didn't want to get into it with him. He has a way of arguing in circles, which really gets on my last nerve.

Day 12. With five games under our belts it looks like this is going to be a great season for the Lakers. Shaq Fu and I have taken to staying up late night at a little bistro in Beachwood Canyon called La Poubelle and talking about the team's potential in the weeks to come. Shaq has turned me on to red wine and good food. In return I got him the new PJ Harvey CD and Shaq says he listens to it nonstop. Unfortunately, I'm finding Shaq to be a bit clingy. He's a cool guy and fun to hang out with but he's kind of eager and not very mellow. Like, the other day we were yardsaling and Shaq goes absolutely berserk over this grubby old Fonzie pillow. I could tell that he was really just trying to impress me with his knowledge of Seventies sitcoms because I told him that he was too young to be Gen X and he's dead-set on proving me wrong.

Day 27. The good news is that the team is in first place. The bad news is that I'm giving Shaq Fu the cold shoulder this week because I heard him bragging to a friend on the team about how he wasn't taking my notes anymore. That's such bullshit. If Shaq doesn't like what I have to say about the way he's playing the game of basketball, then he should be man enough to talk to me about it. I thought we were supposed to be friends or something. And furthermore, he is taking my notes and is obviously trying to take credit for it himself, which I find really lame and, frankly, immature. So, fuck it, I don't want to be his friend right now. Yesterday I proved it. He asked if I wanted to see *Sex, Lies, and Videotape* with him again at the three-dollar theater, and I told him that I was going to Malibu Canyon for a hike and a picnic with Kobe and that he wasn't invited, which I could tell really ticked him off. He acted like he didn't care and said something about how he "loved seeing films alone anyway" but he was obviously bumming. Shaq always puts on this fake smile bit when he's mad at me. I'll start being nice to him again next week.

Day 40. We've fallen back to fourth place, and there's some major tension brewing these days between me and Rick Fox, of all people. Rick's a nice guy but he's Mr. Bandwagon and takes uppers all the time, which gives him major B.O., not to mention an inflated sense of self-worth. The whole thing blew up over the fact that Rick thinks I stole his MP3 player, which couldn't be further from the truth. I told Rick that he could take his accusations and shove them straight up his poop shoot for all I cared. Rick fired back that he didn't have a poop shoot, which led me to believe he'd misunderstood what I meant or that he was born without an asshole, which I highly doubt.

On a happier note, Shaq Diesel and I are back on. Our giggling fits during halftime have become legendary. Like at the Dallas game last week, I farted during Phil Jackson's halftime speech and everybody cracked up. It was really funny. Shaq said it sounded like someone dropped a dictionary on the floor. That really broke people up. Even Phil Jackson. And just when it seemed like we'd stopped giggling, someone would break and we'd all start to crack up again. It was so funny. Shaq told me he laughed so hard his tummy hurt.

Day 48. We've won six games in a row and we're on a roll. Last night a bunch of us went out and partied hearty. A friend of Robert Horry's was having an invite-only thing in Hollywood and we all crashed it. Kobe was so comical. He was like, "Heeere's Johnny." It turns out Samaki Walker is an awesome DJ and was putting on one classic song after another. Everyone was into it. We made him play "Faith" by George (Michael) like five times in a row. Then we made him play the Limp Bizkit version, and a funny debate broke out over which version was better. The whole thing was so comical it would have been an excellent sketch for MADtv we all thought. Then, all of a sudden, "La Isla Bonita" by Madonna comes in over the speakers and the dance floor literally erupts. Before anyone knew it, it was a total rave scene. I couldn't believe it. People were totally doing the cabbage patch and getting into it. Shaq and I were like, "Wow, this is getting out of hand." And then one of the speakers blew, which sucked but we were like, "Fuck it," and we just kept going. Everyone was like, "We'll call it the One Speaker Party! It'll be classic." At one point we all got in a circle and everybody took turns going into the middle and doing a little solo. We were all doing silly dances for each other. Kobe's was kind of corny and awkward but Shaq Fu was so comical because he does the Pee Wee Herman so well. It's totally classic. Everyone said so. Even Phil got into the act with his crazy bad Molly Ringwald dance that she did in *The Breakfast Club*. Then there's this lull and Kobe got this devilish grin on his face and suggested we play I Never, and it was this total nervous energy in the room. And everybody's like, "Ugh, uh…uh…" And I could tell that this girl I'd been talking to wanted to play, and I'm like, "I'll play if you'll play," and she's like, "I'll play if you play," and Kobe's like completely running the show, getting everyone psyched and the next thing I know, it's like this crazy make out scene. Long story short, it's basically like this total orgy, where, like, everyone's making out and kissing and, like, it was nuts. Kobe ends pulling a Technicolor yawn in the backseat of Shaq Diesel's car, which is one part comedy and one part tragedy— for Shaq Fu, that is, who took, like, all night to clean out Kobe's barf.

Day 65. The season is almost over. Every time the season ends there's this real down feeling. Shaq seemed really upset and I could tell that he was wanting to talk about it. Kobe invited us out to Montecito for a roof party at some guy's house he'd met on the road. I wanted to go but it was obvious that Shaq needed some QT, so we told Kobe maybe we'd catch up to him later. Shaq and I waited after practice for everyone to leave and went into the middle of the court and just talked. We must have talked for hours that night. About everything. We talked about God and war, and poetry and love and beauty, and Shaq told me all about what it was like being so tall. And I told him what it was like for me to be so constantly hounded by women. And then at one point we just stopped talking. You could have heard a pin drop. There really wasn't anything to say. We just sat there. Gazing up at the stars—although instead of stars we were looking at gym rafters but they felt like stars. Shaq told me there were a couple of old sleeping bags in the locker room and did I want to camp out on the court that night. I knew I had a long day coming up but I hadn't gone camping in a while and this seemed like a perfect opportunity. We talked more, and eventually got into one of our giggling fits again. Shaq's impersonation of Dana Carvey's impersonation of George Bush is so funny. Then we fell asleep. It seemed like we were up all night but it turns out we fell asleep at about ten o'clock. You lose track of time when you go camping.

Day 87. Last entry. The playoffs are right around the corner and everybody's getting psyched. Shaq and I didn't really tell anyone about our camping trip. It was our little secret. Now when I see Shaq at practice or on the street we say, "Hello." Maybe, "How are you?" Things have definitely changed. But we'll always remember that year and what it was like to be good friends even though it couldn't last forever.

Excerpt and Front and Back Cover Design Specs from My Upcoming Book About Frogs

I am almost finished writing a five-volume work on frogs for a prominent publisher. The project is tentatively titled *Frogs Book* and it's about frogs and what frogs are like and what they do and stuff. Internally, my editors are clamoring for a different title and have suggested simply *Frog Book* because they think that *Frogs Book* is grammatically incorrect and that if I'm going to call it *Frogs Book*, then I should at least put an apostrophe in there so that it reads *Frog's Book* or even *Frogs' Book* but I'm sticking to *Frogs Book* because it was the title that came to me during a morning meditation and I also already had front and back covers made (see following pages for front and back covers specs of *Frogs Book*). The first volume is slated to be eight hundred pages long and so far I've written the first page and a half (quadruple spacing, I admit). The other four volumes I haven't really started yet. And if I'm being honest I'm a bit stressed about it. Eight hundred pages is a lot of pages to write about something you know nothing about.

The following excerpt is a passage from the first chapter of Frogs Book:

CHAPTER ONE: FROGGIES

- Frogs are so cool because they make a funny *ribbit* noise when they talk.
- Fun Frog Fact #1: Frogs can't talk.
- Fun Frog Fact #2: Frogs can jump good.

- French people eat frogs. That's why a derogatory word for French people is *frog*. French people love to eat frogs. Especially they love to eat the frog's legs. That's what "frog's legs" are. Supposedly they taste like chicken. If I were a frog I'd be pissed about this. I'd be like, "Frogs don't taste like chicken! Chicken tastes like frogs!"

Excerpt from My Upcoming Book About Toads

I am also writing a book on toads. Right now I am calling the book *Toads!!!!* I am considering just calling it *Toads!!* or even possibly *Toads!!!* My publishers are insisting on *Toads!* But I think that's so obvious. NO ONE, AND I MEAN NO ONE, IS WORKING WITH FOUR EXCLAMATION POINTS THESE DAYS. But look, these are the kind of luxury problems one would want, I suppose. Right now I'm working my way through the first chapter, and I'll be honest with you: It's not going well. Why? My knowledge of toads, as with frogs, is quite limited. Here's a passage from the opening chapter titled "Toads Are Really Pretty Great."

CHAPTER ONE: TOADS ARE REALLY PRETTY GREAT

Toads are really pretty great. They are really ugly sometimes too but also really cool. They also are horny sometimes but not like the way we get horny sometimes when we're writing on our computer and then suddenly we get horny because all of a sudden we get distracted from writing about toads and start thinking about sex positions and then we have to take a five-minute "break" to do something and then after we've done what we took the break for we wash up and go back to work on our book about toads. Toads are horny in that they kind of like have horns or something. Toads are good jumpers too, I think. Toads are different from frogs in that toads are called toads and frogs aren't called toads. Frogs are called frogs. Another difference between toads and frogs is—[This is all I've got so far.]

I got this note from my editors on the passage you just read.

> *Editor's Note*: Michael, this is not AT ALL what you told us
> you would write about. First of all, you've had almost two years
> to write this book and so far this is all you've submitted to us
> in terms of actual text. We get the impression that you "free-
> associated" on the word "toads" for a few minutes and then
> sent it in. That's not acceptable. Obviously, we will have to
> discuss an extension of deadline, but you really need to start
> generating pages because, as you know, our hope is that this will
> be *the* definitive book on toads and so far it's falling well short
> of that objective. Secondly, there is ABSOLUTELY NO useful
> information here on the subject of toads. While this may seem
> like an "annoying" criticism to *you*, to *us* it is paramount that
> the book really, actually *be* about toads. Thirdly, your digression
> involving "being horny" and "taking a break" seems to imply
> that you went into your bedroom or whatever and jerked off. Do
> I even need to say that this is inappropriate for a book about toads
> and, frankly, rather offensive? Michael, we are all really, truly
> excited to get cracking here on this book about toads with you,
> but there is a genuine concern circulating that you're not working
> as hard on *Toads!* as we had all hoped.

Enraged, I fired back this response.

> *Dear the Editor of* Toads!!!!,
>   *When Saul Bellow sends you his rough manuscript pages is this
> how you treat* him? *I HIGHLY doubt it.* Toads!!!! *or* Toads!, *as
> you INSIST on calling it, is A WORK IN PROGRESS. Maybe
> you think Rome was built in a day? Well guess again! It took
> WEEKS to build Rome. A story: Michelangelo was commissioned
> to make his sculpture of David. He had a huge chunk of marble
> in his studio and for YEARS he just stared at it. He never once
> picked up a chisel. After months of this, one of his apprentices*

said to him, "Michelangelo, what are you doing every day just staring at the chunk of marble?" And do you know what he said? He said, "I'm working." That's what I'm doing too. I'm staring at a big chunk of marble every day and somewhere hidden inside that big chunk of marble is Toads!!!! and once it reveals itself to me it will flow forth. What's my point? My point is that Toads!!!! will be written when Toads!!!! is READY to be written. So until that time I suggest that you think twice about what you say to me because ultimately it's all of the people who want to read about toads who will suffer the most.

Yours Truly,
Michael Showalter

TOADS!!!!

A NEW BOOK FROM ACCLAIMED AUTHOR AND FROG EXPERT MICHAEL SHOWALTER

ADVANCE PRAISE FOR MICHAEL SHOWALTER'S *TOADS!!!!*

"THE TOAD VOICE OF HIS GENERATION."
–JAY MCINERNEY, AUTHOR

"A TOAD BOOK FOR ANYONE WHO KNOWS WHAT TOADS ARE."
–JIM JARMUSCH, FILMMAKER

"*TOADS!!!!* IS TO TOADS WHAT *FROGS BOOK* WAS FOR FROGS."
–JULIAN SCHNABEL, ARTIST

"I READ EVERY PAGE OF *TOADS!!!!*"
–SOFIA COPPOLA, FILMMAKER

"TOAD-ALLY AWESOME!"
–DAVID BYRNE, MUSICIAN

"SHOWALTER'S TOADS PROSE IS AUTHENTIC."
–BRET EASTON ELLIS, AUTHOR

"*TOADS!!!!* GRABS YOU AND NEVER LETS GO."
–TAMA JANOWITZ, AUTHOR

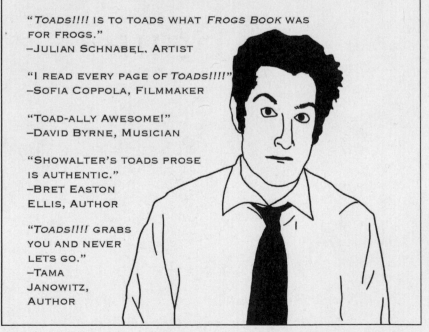

The Original First Paragraph

"*This whole thing started very innocently. It was January 2008. It was a dark and slushy January in Brooklyn. The air was freezing cold, like breathing popsicles. When I walked outside, my heather gray winter beard would be encased in a thin sheet of ice. It was so cold that I had to chop my wood indoors. If I chopped my wood outside, my fingers would get brittle and break off. My electric blanket was set permanently to the number 20, which meant that my bed was hot enough to bake muffins in. And by muffins I also mean scones, biscuits, and loaves (loafs?) of bread. If you had a job, you'd go to work in the morning and by noon the sun would have set. I know this because when I woke up at one o'clock in the afternoon every day, I'd call my friends with jobs and they'd tell me about it. In the sun's place would fall an unforgiving blackness that hung over the city like a big bag of eggplant.*"

Editor's Note: It's *loaves*.
Response to Editor's Note: That's all?

Editor's Note: What do you mean?
Response to Editor's Note: Did you like it?

Editor's Note: Not really, no.
Response to Editor's Note: Why?

Editor's Note: It makes it sound like you're a lumberjack or something. You don't have a beard. You don't chop wood.
Response to Editor's Note: Creative license, Ben.

Editor's Note: What about that thing about when you peed on yourself? I liked that more.

FAQs (Frequently Asked Questions)

Q: What is the meaning of life?
A: The meaning of life is to live.

Q: Does God exist?
A: Sure.

Q: Which came first, the chicken or the egg?
A: The chicken. I read about it in the *New York Times*. They said the chicken.

Q: Beatles or Stones, who's better?
A: Beatles. Stones are really good, though.

Q: Why is Meryl Streep in every movie?
A: She is the only actress in the world.

Q: Does the early bird really get the worm?
A: Depends on when the worm shows up.

Q: How much wood could a woodchuck chuck?
A: Consistency of the wood is a factor, also the energy level of the woodchuck, also not sure what *chuck* means? Is it a verb?

Q: Is there life on other planets?
A: No.

Q: Does Bigfoot exist?

A: Yes, however he does not, as rumored, have big feet. He has tiny feet.

Q: Is anyone really bisexual?

A: Yes. All women are bisexual and like threesomes with a guy and another woman.

Q: Was Jesus black?

A: Very.

Q: Is Elvis still alive?

A: No, but his memory will live on forever.

Q: Should pot be legalized?

A: Yes, but pot stickers and all forms of dumplings should be outlawed.

Q: My boyfriend wants to try anal. What should I do?

A: Dunno. It's kind of up to you.

Q: I masturbate a lot. Is that bad for me?

A: If you're masturbating on a clump of asbestos, yes.

Q: How do I get an acting agent?

A: Get cast in a big movie.

Q: How do I get cast in a big movie?

A: Get an acting agent.

Q: What's the capital of Rhode Island?

A: Who cares?

Q: What's the fastest land mammal?
A: The cheetah.

Q: What's the fastest water mammal?
A: The duck.

Q: What's the slowest land mammal?
A: My cat Sally.

Q: It hurts when I bend my knee?
A: Don't bend your knee.

Q: Why do wolves howl at the moon?
A: They are communicating with God.

Q: Do lady ogres have a vagina?
A: Yes. Three.

Q: Is there such a thing as love at first sight?
A: According to the movies, yes.

Q: What is happiness?
A: A full belly and a nap.

Q: Do you like Sting's solo stuff?
A: No.[14] His Police stuff was way better. His solo stuff is cheesy.

Q: Who is your greatest comic inspiration?
A: Buster Keaton.

Q: Really?
A: Albert Brooks.

14. Love Sting's solo stuff.

Q: Really?
A: John Ritter.

Q: Really?
A: Garfield.

Q: Thought so.
Q: Are you really a dick? I read somewhere online that you were a dick.
A: I can get a little panicky in social situations. People think I'm being a dick when in reality I'm just uncomfortable.

Q: But you're a performer?
A: So was J. D. Salinger. He was a famous recluse.

Q: He wasn't a performer.
A: Right. Obviously.

Q: He was a writer.
A: That's what I'm saying. He was a writer.

Q: You didn't say that.
A: I was testing you.

Q: I'm you, though.
A: What?

Q: I'm you.
A: Oh really? Then what's my middle name?

Q: I'm supposed to be the one asking the questions.
A: Don't know it, huh?

Q: It's English.
A: Huh. Maybe you are me.

Q: I know I'm you.
A: But if you're me, then who am I?

Q: You're also me.
A: Fuck off!

Q: We're the same person.
A: We are?

Q: Yes. You're writing the questions and the answers.
A: I am?

Q: Yes.
A: Huh. That's trippy.

Sincere, Not Silly, Thank You Page

Ben Greenberg, my favorite book editor that I've ever had, without whom I'd never have had this opportunity which I enjoyed so much having in the first place [Structure? Consider changing]; Michelle Walson for helping me so much on this book with her fabulous ideas and encouragements! My mom and dad and sister for being the best parents and sister in the world; my better half, Kalin, who makes me laugh every day, even when I'm feeling down in the dumps; Stephanie Isaacson for swooping in at the last minute and making all the pictures look so good; everybody at Grand Central who helped make this book; Peter Principato, Jay Gassner, Josh Katz and Keya Kheyatian, Tom Carr, and Mike Shutello; Eugene Mirman and Julie Smith for letting me read it out loud in front of people; God/Universal Soul/Buddha (pick your word).